Praise for Journey to Freedom

"The Church is starving from a lack of teaching that connects us to Christ and builds our foundation in Him. This is why I am so thrilled with Journey to Freedom. It is a marvelous discipleship tool that can inspire you in your walk with God and help you overcome every personal struggle. I hope you will make this part of your daily devotions. It is strong meat that boosts your spiritual diet!"

J. Lee Grady, director, The Mordecai Project;
former editor, *Charisma* magazine

"This comprehensive teaching about the ways, works and words of the living God invites us deeper into intimacy with Him. It is personal and practical, pastoral and prophetic, encouraging and educating, appealing and revealing. It is Christ-centered, Holy Spirit–empowered and inspired. I love it! I need it! I am going to use it! So should you!"

Stuart McAlpine, pastor, Christ Our Shepherd Church,
Capitol Hill, Washington, D.C.

"If you are serious about wanting to experience the deep truths of God in your life, then this is possibly the most relevant and pertinent tool of ministry I have discovered. It is insightful, challenging and informative. I heartily endorse this tool of transformation and challenge you to read it and prepare for change!"

Alistair P. Petrie, executive director, Partnership Ministries

"An amazing array of information that is at once biblical, practical and comprehensive. To find a guide like this, covering the simplest truths of the faith to the deepest and most profound, is like discovering buried treasure—simply outstanding!"

David Kyle Foster, director, Mastering Life Ministries,
Franklin, Tennessee; producer, *Pure Passion* TV program

"An incredible opportunity for the Body of Christ to help people grow into strong, mature Christians. Simple, understandable yet profound teaching that anyone interested in finding fullness in the Lord can easily access. The materials are presented in a practical way with opportunities for personal application."

Ruth Ruibal, president, Julio C. Ruibal Ministries, Colombia

Testimonies from some who applied the Journey to Freedom teaching in their lives when first published online

"It has changed my life forever. These past twelve months have been the most fulfilling and exciting experience I have had in my walk with the Lord."

"My relationship with God is going from strength to strength—I just love it."

"It has been a lifeline. It held me safe while Father God touched the broken places."

"I so long for everyone to experience what I'm now experiencing."

"The most important thing I've ever done—it's reality!"

"Truly life-transforming—and I still have a ways to go!"

"In faith, honesty and obedience, my heavy burden was lifted and I was set free. What joy!"

"The relief from the hold of sin was wonderful—worth every pain and all the tears I've shed!"

"Now I know I have a Father in heaven. The lie of the enemy has been broken."

"The teaching is extraordinary and beautiful. It all makes perfect sense. I'm amazed at the things I am learning. I wish I'd had this when I first became a Christian."

"My formerly derailed destiny in life is being put back on the fast track!"

"Challenging and provoking. God is using it to wonderfully transform my life."

"Inspired and inspirational. The teaching is astounding and has opened up a whole new experience for me in my Christian journey."

"I now believe I have a destiny and a future that I didn't have before. Miracles *do* happen!"

"Excellent and brilliant foundational teaching for every Christian."

BUILDING ON THE ROCK

JOURNEY TO FREEDOM

BUILDING ON THE ROCK

Understanding the Gospel *and* Living It Out

PETER HORROBIN

Chosen

a division of Baker Publishing Group
Minneapolis, Minnesota

© 2019 by Peter Horrobin

Published by Chosen Books
11400 Hampshire Avenue South
Bloomington, Minnesota 55438
www.chosenbooks.com

Chosen Books is a division of
Baker Publishing Group, Grand Rapids, Michigan

Printed in the United States of America

All rights reserved. No part of this publication may be reproduced, stored in a retrieval system, or transmitted in any form or by any means—for example, electronic, photocopy, recording—without the prior written permission of the publisher. The only exception is brief quotations in printed reviews.

ISBN 978-0-8007-9945-8

Library of Congress Cataloging-in-Publication Control Number: 2019021619

Originally published under the title Journey to Freedom, Book 1, Building on the Rock by Sovereign World Ltd, Ellel Ministries International, Ellel, Lancaster, Lancashire, LA2 0HN, United Kingdom.

Published digitally as *Ellel 365*.

Unless otherwise indicated, Scripture quotations are from the Holy Bible, New International Version®. NIV®. Copyright © 1973, 1978, 1984, 2011 by Biblica, Inc.™ Used by permission of Zondervan. All rights reserved worldwide. www.zondervan.com. The "NIV" and "New International Version" are trademarks registered in the United States Patent and Trademark Office by Biblica, Inc.™

Scripture quotations labeled AMPC are from the Amplified® Bible (AMPC), copyright © 1954, 1958, 1962, 1964, 1965, 1987 by The Lockman Foundation. Used by permission. www.Lockman.org

Scripture quotations labeled ESV Scripture quotations are from The Holy Bible, English Standard Version® (ESV®), copyright © 2001 by Crossway, a publishing ministry of Good News Publishers. Used by permission. All rights reserved. ESV Text Edition: 2016

Scripture quotations labeled GNT are from the Good News Translation in Today's English Version-Second Edition. Copyright © 1992 by American Bible Society. Used by permission. Scripture quotations labeled KJV are from the King James Version of the Bible.

Scripture quotations labeled NKJV are from the New King James Version®. Copyright © 1982 by Thomas Nelson. Used by permission. All rights reserved.

Personal stories of individuals in this book are used by permission. Identifying details of certain individuals have been changed to protect their privacy.

In keeping with biblical principles of creation stewardship, Baker Publishing Group advocates the responsible use of our natural resources. As a member of the Green Press Initiative, our company uses recycled paper when possible. The text paper of this book is composed in part of post-consumer waste.

Cover design by Emily Weigel

CONTENTS

Introduction   9

Stage 1 My Life in God's Hands

1. The "God-Box"   17
2. My Life—Made for Living   24
3. My Place in God's World   30
4. My Destiny in God's Hands   35
5. My Security in God's Love   41

Stage 2 Vital Foundations

6. Eternity in the Heart of Man   49
7. The Father's Heart for You and Me   54
8. Sin—Rebellion That Separates from God   59
9. Jesus—Savior and Friend of Sinners   68
10. Holy Spirit—Empowerment for God's People   75

Stage 3 The Bible—My Guide for Life

11. God's Amazing Letter to the Human Race   85
12. Feeding on the Living Bread   92
13. Taking It All In   100

14. Guidance for Daily Living   108
15. Encouragement and Inspiration at All Times   116

Stage 4 The Vital Breath of Prayer

16. Prayer—The Christian's Vital Breath   127
17. The Lord's Prayer—Worship and Adoration   136
18. The Lord's Prayer—Kingdom Authority and Trust   145
19. The Lord's Prayer—Forgiveness   154
20. The Lord's Prayer—Crying Out to God   164

Stage 5 Healed for a Purpose

21. What Does Healing Mean?   175
22. Why Do I Need Healing?   184
23. Generational Issues   192
24. Things That Have Happened to Me   202
25. What Have I Done?   210

Stage 6 Equipped to Serve

26. Healing for Disciples   223
27. Healing for the Inner Man   231
28. Set Free to Serve   238
29. Ready for Action   247
30. The Joy of Serving God   254

Now Read On . . .   263

INTRODUCTION

BUILDING ON THE ROCK

"If you hold to my teaching, you are really my disciples. Then you will know the truth, and the truth will set you free."

John 8:31–32

In over thirty years of ministry, I have witnessed firsthand how the Lord has brought deep healing, restoration and freedom to even the most hurting and broken people. JOURNEY TO FREEDOM contains the life-transforming keys from God's Word that will enable you to enjoy personal transformation and freedom one step at a time.

The original edition of JOURNEY TO FREEDOM was published online under the title *Ellel 365*. It provided a whole year of teaching and training in 365 daily units. The material in this book has been tested thoroughly and used by thousands of people within most of the nations of the world. There are many wonderful stories of how God used these daily lessons to transform and heal people's lives as they joined in the adventure of faith that is at the heart of JOURNEY TO FREEDOM. Along with the JOURNEY TO FREEDOM books, the online edition of *Ellel 365*, which is being reintroduced, has also been updated.

While thousands of people have enjoyed reading the lessons of *Ellel 365* online, there is still a large body of people who prefer being able to hold traditional books in their hands. These volumes, therefore, have been produced in response to popular demand. Whether you are studying JOURNEY TO FREEDOM online or reading it as a series of books, it is the same God who will be there with you along the way—on a journey that is both a pilgrimage and an adventure.

This is a journey through which God can transform your life one step at a time as you understand and apply each chapter's scriptural teaching. I do not write these words lightly—I believe them with every part of my being. I *know* God changes people's lives. I have seen it happen. I *know* He brings healing and freedom to those who are struggling. I *know* God is interested in every detail of our lives. I *know* He wants to set us free from the hold of the enemy. And I *know* He wants to see you living in the destiny He has prepared for you.

We serve a truly awesome God who is as real and active today as He was in all of the stories that we read in the Bible (see Hebrews 13:8). I am looking forward to sharing some of these stories with you. They are powerful testimonies of what the Lord has done in people's lives as His truth has become established in their hearts.

Many have been set free from long-term physical and psychological conditions, addictions and generational curses. Deep wounds of abuse and rejection have been healed by our gentle Father God. Identities that have been crushed and sometimes burdened with guilt and shame have been restored, and relationships have been healed and repaired.

People have been healed from the consequences of deep trauma. Wounds have been touched by the Lord, and strongholds of the enemy have been broken. The fruits of bitterness have melted away through love and forgiveness. Debilitating fears have been discarded and replaced with courage and trust—many beautiful stories of life-transformation by a God who cares passionately for you and for me.

Strong and Lasting Foundations

All buildings need strong and lasting foundations. Without solid groundwork buildings will have a limited number of years of usefulness, or they may collapse dangerously. In a similar way, your life needs

Introduction

to have strong and lasting spiritual foundations. When your life is built on solid foundations, you are able to enter into the calling and destiny that God has reserved for you. JOURNEY TO FREEDOM will help you establish strong foundations as a preparation for all that God has for you in the rest of your life.

I am excited about the faith journey we are embarking on together. A wealth of vital material has been made available to you. You will be able to make this journey at the pace that is right for you with the freedom to move on from one chapter to the next whenever you feel ready. But may I encourage you to start at the beginning and not overlook or skip any of the chapters? Each and every one contains vital life-giving material.

It may be tempting to flip through the book and dip into later chapters, especially on subjects in which you have a special interest. But as we have already established, you cannot construct a safe building without the foundations being in place. The foundations that will be built into your life through the early chapters of the book could be of critical importance to you.

The most genuine and lasting works of personal transformation that I have witnessed have often come as part of an ongoing pilgrimage with the Lord. This is how the Holy Spirit works in our lives in order to establish godly order—one step at a time. For many of us, the struggles in our lives are not going to be fixed in a day.

We may cry out, "Heal me, Lord," but for most of us, God does not heal us dramatically or through instant transformation. He heals us by working carefully and tenderly in our hearts in the hidden areas that we may have tried hard to ignore or to discard. Paul's instruction to the Galatians was to restore people gently (see Galatians 6:1). When our heavenly Father brings His truth into our innermost beings, He establishes strong and lasting foundations through which He brings stability, deep healing and wholeness.

Sometimes people need help with their personal healing journeys, or they need training in how to help others. It is for this reason that Ellel Ministries established training and ministry centers in various places and countries. The first center was at Ellel Grange, a large country house in northwest England. In old English the word *ellel* means "all hail" or "praise God." In Hebrew it could mean "going toward God." It was a very appropriate word to use for the whole work that has become known worldwide as Ellel Ministries. The first Ellel Center in the U.S.A. was established in Florida. There are also centers in Canada near Kingston, Ontario, and near Calgary, Alberta.

Our prayer for the local church, however, is that every church should be a center of healing and training where believers can grow in their faith and know God's healing. It is my prayer that JOURNEY TO FREEDOM will also help local leaders bring God's healing to their people.

Many of the people I meet and pray with come to our centers because of the unwelcome fruit they see in their lives, such as depression, relationship breakdowns, sicknesses, financial crisis or ruin, insomnia, addictions, pornography, obesity or many other problems with which people struggle.

This causes them to cry out to the Lord for healing of the symptoms. However, the roots of the problems can go a whole lot deeper. The pain they are experiencing often comes from issues such as despair, fear, anxiety, or a sense of failure and unworthiness. They feel guilty and unfulfilled, angry, lonely, hopeless or have a lack of identity. They may even feel like they have no reason to live.

You may be an expert at covering up your struggles, or you may try to function normally and ignore the inner limping that has become part of your everyday life. The Lord, however, longs to repair deep areas of your heart. He wants not to only deal with the fruit seen on the surface or do temporary repair work of what you are struggling with today, He wants to free you.

Jesus said, "If the Son sets you free, you will be free indeed" (John 8:36). Unless He heals the foundation of our lives, we can never really become the people He created us to be.

Truth and Reality

On each stage of this journey as you read and take in one chapter at a time, I believe the Lord will begin to build new foundations of truth and revelation into your heart. We will start at the beginning by taking a realistic look at who you are in God and what your relationship with Him is. We will learn much from the lives of others as we absorb the invaluable lessons contained within God's Word.

JOURNEY TO FREEDOM is not a Bible study aimed at making you more knowledgeable as a Christian. The heart of this journey is to learn how to apply both the truths of God's Word and His character deep into your being. Then He can transform the hidden depths of who you are into the beautiful creation He intended you to be. It is all for His glory and not for ours. My prayer is that by the enabling power of the Holy Spirit you will have the courage and the willingness to allow the Lord to shine His truth into every area of your being.

It is easy to hide the true motives of our hearts and to deceive ourselves, but it is only as we are real before the One who created us that we can allow Him to make those essential differences in our lives. Psalm 51:6 says, "You desire truth in the inward parts, and in the hidden part You will make me to know wisdom" (NKJV). Jesus said, "Then you will know the truth, and the truth will set you free" (John 8:32).

At the very beginning of your journey to freedom, I encourage you to commit your life afresh to the Lord and give Him permission to shine His light of truth deep into your heart:

Father God, thank You so much for who You are, for Your love and for Your desire to restore my life so that I can walk in the destiny prepared for me from the very beginning. I pray that You will show me the areas in which I have been hurt and need healing. Help me to see the places where I have gotten it wrong and need forgiveness and restoration. Help me to give You first place in every area of my being as I learn how to apply the truth of Your Word in my life. I invite You to be Lord of every area of my being. In Jesus' name, Amen.

On a Practical Note

The original online *Ellel 365* program contained five teachings, one for each weekday. On the sixth day there was a review of what had been covered in the previous five days, and on the seventh day there was a devotional reading. The review and the devotional are omitted from this printed version of JOURNEY TO FREEDOM, but the structure of the original material has been retained. You can follow the same weekly pattern through a whole year. One difference you might notice is that each week's teaching of the original *Ellel 365* is now referred to as *stage* in this book form of JOURNEY TO FREEDOM.

You may prefer to work through the book at your own speed to suit your own personal situation, but whatever pattern you choose, I encourage you to persevere. Some of the most profound testimonies from *Ellel 365* were from people who did just that, and at the end of the journey they were amazed at all that God had done. I believe passionately in the God of miracles, but I also recognize that some miracles take place over a period of time. When I see the extraordinary transformation that God has wrought one step at a time, I stand amazed at the way the God of miracles has been at work.

I would love to hear what God does in your life on your own journey to freedom. You can share your testimony by writing to me at peter.horrobin@ellel.org. I will look forward to hearing from you.

STAGE 1

MY LIFE IN GOD'S HANDS

God is my security—I can trust and depend completely on Him.

THE "GOD-BOX" 1

All of us had a beginning. None of us have memories of the precise moment we were conceived, but it was at that moment God gave us life and our earthly pilgrimages began.

God breathed into you His breath of life (your human spirit) and you became a living soul (see Genesis 2:7). The physical cells began to divide, and you started to grow. Your spirit, soul and body were all present from those earliest moments—they are what makes you a human being.

On your *birth-day* you began life separated from your mother. From babyhood you progressed through a time of being cared for, and eventually you grew into adulthood. Through the passage of time you became the person you are today.

Although you are a unique creation in God, what you look like was influenced by your family's genetic history. The person God created you to be (the person living within your body) has been influenced by the many experiences of your life from the time of your birth.

What you have chosen to do, the way others have treated you and the way you have responded to these events have all contributed to molding you into the person you now are. Your physical appearance bears the impressions and scars of your life's events—both the good and the bad.

When I have to wait at an airport or a railway station, I look at the faces of people passing by. Some are happy while others are sad, and it is often easy to see the emotional and spiritual scars that people are carrying. The face was designed by God to express our feelings, and it shows the consequences of what we have been through.

The majority of people make their way through life without any knowledge of God or how He could help and heal them. But this was not God's original intention.

God's Plan for the Human Race

It was God's plan that children would be brought up in the nurture of the Lord (see Ephesians 6:4; Proverbs 22:6). God intended that children would learn from their parents everything about Him and what it means to live as human beings.

With this method, learning about the knowledge of God from day one would be part of our everyday lives, and growing up would be a good experience. Little by little we would learn about the nature and ways of God from our parents, because *their* parents had learned the truth about God from their parents and so on down the generations.

We also find this method within the Church through discipleship. Spiritual moms and dads are to train young ones in the faith (see 1 Corinthians 4:14–17). God's plan was that human beings would grow up to enjoy every aspect of their humanity in loving relationships with God and with each other.

The Reality

Reality, however, tells us that the world is very different from the ideal that God intended originally. We only need to see the headlines in one issue of any national newspaper to see plenty of evidence that lives are not being lived according to God's intentions. In many places normal family life has almost disintegrated. Something has gone seriously wrong.

We see violence, stealing, ungodly sexual relationships, war, drugs, betrayal and a thousand other things that God did not plan or intend for us. We are now seeing some of the evil things prophesied in the Word of God being fulfilled before our very eyes, even to the extent that evil is being called good and good is being called evil (see Isaiah 5:20).

In most countries of the world scriptural morality is no longer an acceptable basis for law, and every flavor of occult or perverted sexual activity is acceptable for both entertainment and personal involvement. A large percentage of the films being produced by the movie industry are about horror, demonic power or explicit sex. Tragically, this is what the deceived heart of man wants to watch. All of this confirms that the world is in an unholy mess and is a million miles away from what God planned or intended for us.

It is important for you to see how the world got into its present mess to understand that God has an amazing rescue plan for humanity (see Isaiah 61:1–4; John 10:10). You will discover how He wants to heal and restore you so that you can walk in the wonderful destiny He has planned (see Joel 2:25–27; Jeremiah 29:11).

God's Jigsaw Puzzle

A jigsaw puzzle is a picture that is cut into many different pieces that fit together, each of which carries a part of the whole picture. It often comes in a box with a picture on the lid showing the completed puzzle.

God has revealed Himself to mankind in the most wonderful of pictures. Within Scripture, the revelation begins in the Garden of Eden and concludes in the book of Revelation with images of heaven. From Genesis to Revelation, we see a picture unfolding of foundational truths about God and man.

Each truth is like a piece of an incredible jigsaw puzzle. Put them all together, and you have an amazing understanding of the nature and character of God and of what God's best is for mankind.

Our "God-Box"

The *God-box* is the name I have given to the "spiritual container" into which we put all of the bits of spiritual knowledge that we acquire on life's journey. Since our conception we have been learning new things and putting pieces of spiritual understanding into our God-boxes. They are like pieces of a jigsaw puzzle.

Everyone has encountered different life experiences—from childhood through adulthood—so everyone's God-boxes are filled differently. If a person's only source of opinions is their own life experience, then no two people can ever be in full agreement about what they think about God. The pieces of the puzzle in your personal God-box will never be the same as anyone else's.

That is why, for example, there are many different religions in the world. Each one is an expression of people's attempt to find God based on their own accumulated knowledge and experience. These expressions will always be incomplete and inadequate.

As a child I loved doing jigsaw puzzles; however, a puzzle with pieces missing could never be completed. It was frustrating and disappointing to have worked hard and yet not to be able to complete the picture. Lack of sufficient knowledge and spiritual understanding is a problem that we all face. If we try to depend on our own understanding (see Proverbs 3:5–6), we will always have inadequate knowledge of the truth about God. There will be important pieces missing from our God-boxes, and we will not be able to complete the picture of truth about either God or man.

But there is another problem we have to face as well.

Extra Pieces

One day I came across a particularly difficult jigsaw puzzle that had some extra pieces. The extra pieces looked as though they were part of the picture on the lid of the box, but they did not fit anywhere in the puzzle.

They had been added deliberately by the manufacturers to make the jigsaw puzzle even more difficult. If you did put one of these extra pieces into the puzzle, it made the rest of the puzzle impossible to do.

This illustrates the sort of difficulties we all face when trying to understand the truth about God. From the moment we were conceived we have been acquiring many different pieces of information about life. We have been putting these into our God-boxes as pieces of our spiritual jigsaw puzzles.

Some of the pieces have been accurate and fit in the puzzle; however, many of our pieces of spiritual understanding have been acquired from others—especially our parents—as we have grown up. These pieces include many false beliefs. When we add pieces to our boxes that do not actually fit in the puzzle, the end result is that we cannot create an accurate representation of the picture on the box cover. When we try, we end up with a skewed image of God.

I once prayed with a lady who struggled terribly with the belief that God was a Father who loved her. I later found out that her human father had beat her regularly. As a result, she believed that all fathers were cruel—including Father God.

Some people have difficulty praying. They cannot believe that God has time for them. Many such people had fathers who were too busy with their own lives and did not have time for their children. The message in their God-box says, "God does not have time for me, either."

Many people have been introduced to beliefs associated with a false religion. Because their parents were Buddhists, for example, they have become Buddhists. Or because they had a very superstitious parent or grandparent, they have absorbed these false beliefs as their own. Older people can open the door to the next generation to many and varied New Age beliefs and occult practices. Experiences like these have the effect of sewing lies into our God-boxes.

Young children cannot differentiate between the good and bad pieces of information they have received from significant adults in their lives. It is all truth to them. When we believe things from a young age that are false, those things can influence the way we think and what we believe today.

The Real Situation

The fact is that all of us have had truth and error, good and bad poured into us throughout our lives. As a result, most of us are very confused. We can have huge gaps in our understanding of real truth, and we can have many extra pieces of spiritual knowledge that have nothing whatsoever to do with God. Our images of God have been distorted by experiences within our lives.

It is important that you take a hard look at yourself and let God show you any areas of unbelief or wrong belief that might have influenced your relationship with Him or stood in the way of your growth or healing (see Psalm 51:6; Psalm 139:23–24).

God's Answer

The answer to this problem can be found in Jesus. One of the reasons that Jesus came was to show us what God is really like (see John 14:7–11).

Before Jesus, the human race had been trying to fit all of their jigsaw pieces together to form pictures—but they made no sense. They could not tell truth from error. They needed a picture that they could use to compare to the pieces in their God-boxes so they could get rid of the ones that did not fit into their puzzles.

Jesus is the picture we need. We can model our lives after His life. The more we become like Him, the more effective and blessed our earthly and eternal lives will be (see 2 Corinthians 3:18). The progressive revelation of Scripture finds its total fulfillment in Jesus (see Luke 4:21). He is the ultimate gift of God to the human race (see John 3:16). It is very important that we know Him as He really is, for He is the key to all healing and to finding our God-given destinies (see John 10:10).

As you take one step at a time on your personal journey to freedom, you will see that not only did Jesus come to save you from the consequences of sin (see 1 Timothy 1:15), but He also came to give you an example of the nature and character of God (see John 14:6–11). He came to teach you how you can have a healed and restored relationship with the Father (see 2 Corinthians 6:18).

As you walk with Jesus in the ways of God, you will experience His transforming power changing you to be more like Him. You will be transformed by the truth and freedom that is only found in Him (see John 8:32).

SUMMARY

Our lives were gifts from God, but through the years we have all developed distorted views of the nature and character of the God who made us. How much we must be missing out on as a result. To get back to a right understanding of God, we will need to identify and deal with those beliefs that are not of God, and we will need to complete the picture of truth as we look at Jesus.

PRAYER

Thank You, Lord, for the privilege of being part of Your creation. As I start moving forward one step at a time, help me to appreciate all You have provided for me, and help me desire to love and serve You all my days. In Jesus' name, Amen.

MY LIFE—MADE FOR LIVING

For many years I have enjoyed restoring old cars. My heart seems to beat a little bit faster when I see a grand old car of days gone by still on the road. I have had many wonderful adventures with cars bearing names that many of you may have never heard of such as Riley, Lagonda and Alvis.

Even today I have a car in the garage that is older than I am. But very few people would be able to drive it. Not because it is hard to drive, but because no one has taught them how to start the engine. You cannot jump into the driver's seat and turn the key—there is none. There are a few basic steps that must be carried out before the engine will burst into life. Without knowing these basics, the car is useless.

God's Order for Living

In a similar way, many people today have not learned the basics of God's order for living. As a result, they are unable to do what God intended for their lives. They have not discovered that their lives were truly made for living.

In these early sections of our journey to freedom, I am putting some important foundational principles in place. Many years of experience of ministering to people across the world have proven time and time again how important this is.

What is obvious to some people is not obvious to others. And for many people, reminders of vital foundations have been the keys that opened doors to miracles in their lives.

I remember a man who had two theological degrees telling me that it was only when we went through these foundations together that he really understood what the cross was all about. That changed everything for him.

You Are a Miracle

Take a look at your hands and marvel at the way they are made. The fingers and the joints are designed perfectly to carry out all of the essential tasks of life. Imagine what eating would be like if you had no hands to prepare the food, to pick it up or to put it in your mouth.

Then run the end of your fingers gently over different surfaces. Your fingers are so sensitive that even with your eyes closed you can tell what you are touching.

Take a deep breath and thank God for the oxygen in the air. Imagine what is happening in your lungs as the oxygen crosses into your bloodstream and is carried to every part of your body, bringing life to all your vital organs. Without oxygen you would die quickly.

Every part of your body has been designed carefully by an incredible genius—the one we call our loving Creator God. As the psalmist said, "I am fearfully and wonderfully made" (Psalm 139:14).

With your eyes you can see. With your ears you can hear. With your nose you can smell. And with your tongue you can taste. Every one of your senses is a miracle of operational genius.

With your mouth you can both speak and eat. Your digestive system processes food, extracts the good nutrients, stores energy as fat and eliminates waste. Your legs, arms, muscles and bones help you get around and accomplish tasks. When you sleep, everything shuts down for seven or eight hours so that you can recover your strength for a new day.

Yes, you are a miracle, and your body is the most amazing of machines. But you are more than a machine.

More Than a Machine

I am typing these notes on a computer with those amazing fingers God gave me. The computer is also a marvelous machine, but it does not do anything unless I correctly set up the operating programs, type instructions on the keyboard or click my mouse.

A computer, like any other machine, requires an operator to use it according to the maker's instructions. Without an operator, the computer will sit on the desk and produce nothing. And if you do not know how to obey the instructions, even the most expensive computer will cause you endless frustration as it refuses to do what you want. I know from hard experience.

In a similar way, you are the operator of the machine called your body. Unless you give your body some instructions, it will function as an unused computer. An unused computer has great potential, but it produces absolutely nothing.

Machines are also made to be used in a certain way. If you misuse a machine, you will damage its operating mechanisms. Before long it will become useless. In the same way, if you misuse your body, the time will come when it will cease to function properly. Life will come grinding to a halt.

The computer was designed to be highly productive when working together in harmony with its operator. There seems to be no limit to what can be done from the keyboard. I have written an important letter to a friend and sent it by email. Then I ordered a birthday present for my grandson from an online store. After which I looked at a news website to see what was happening around the world.

This one machine programmed and operated all of these different things in a matter of minutes. But I had to give the computer the correct instructions and tell it what to do.

Your body was designed in a similar way to be highly productive. I have already done many things today with my own personal machine—my body. After a night's sleep I got my body out of bed and took on some fuel (breakfast) before taking the dog for a walk. I then sat down at the computer to do all the things I told you about. My body and I worked together as a unit to achieve all that I had planned for the day.

Who Are You?

While most people will recognize you by the shape of your body, you are more than your body.

A day will come when your bodily machine will run out of its capacity to cope with the pressures of daily living. Your machine will then cease to function, and the world will say that you have died. But nothing could be further from the truth. You do not die when your body ceases to function.

When you reach that point, you will discover firsthand that your body is, in reality, only a machine—a temporary home—and that you have moved on to a different realm of existence.

There is life after death, as Jesus proved to us when He was raised from the dead. Your soul and your spirit will continue to live beyond the grave. The nature and quality of that life will be related directly to the choices you made while living on earth (see 1 Corinthians 3:12–15; Matthew 6:19–20).

Later we will look more closely at the nature of both God and man. We will learn more about how God intended our souls and spirits to work together in harmony within our bodies so that we can be the people God intended us to be.

Life Is for Living

You are a person in your own right. Your earthly body is a temporary home—not an eternal residence. On earth, you and your body are inseparable. Your body gives you a visible identity, and it enables you to function as a human being. God has created you for a purpose, and He loves you. You are special to Him. You were made for living.

But what does that mean? It means certainly more than functioning as a machine. Jesus said, "I have come that they may have life, and have it to the full" (John 10:10). Jesus was not talking about mere existence.

To comprehend this fully, we will need to understand why the world is in such a mess. Jesus came to rescue us from the trouble that humans had gotten themselves into because of their rebellion against God and their sinful choices (see John 3:17). Those choices have produced a harvest of pain, bitterness and suffering.

How can we live life to the full when we are held back by the chains of ungodly choices made by both ourselves and others, including our ancestors? These are important questions that we will need to address.

Yes, we can look forward to eternity in heaven, and that will be a wonderful escape from the hardships of life on earth. But I do not think that escape is all Jesus was referring to when He talked about giving us the opportunity to live our lives to the fullest.

You were made for living—here on earth as well as throughout eternity. But you also have an enemy, the enemy of souls. Satan does not want you to enter into the blessings God has prepared for you. Satan wants you to be dysfunctional spiritually and to never know the joy of real life (see John 10:10). God has a better plan for your life (see Ephesians 2:10).

Before man sinned, he was able to enjoy the fullness of life in fellowship and relationship with God. But because of sin, man became separated from God (see Genesis 3:8–10). Fullness of life means living in relationship with our Creator (see Ephesians 3:17–19). Outside of God we can never live our lives to the fullest extent. Our potential will always be limited by a breakdown in our relationships with the One who made us.

We may be able to use the gifts and abilities that God gave us, but outside of a restored relationship with God, the damage caused by sin can never be healed. And no matter how successful a person might appear to be, outside of God that success will never satisfy his or her desire for relationship with the Creator.

Living lives to the fullest means living our lives in restored relationships with Father God and discovering how He transforms us from the inside out. That way we can become the children of God He planned from the beginning. Only in that place will we truly know the joy of the Lord. That joy will become our strength for daily living (see Nehemiah 8:10).

Today is a good day for you to decide to give God first place in every area of your life. As you travel step by step on this journey to freedom, allow Him to restore you to be like Him.

SUMMARY

God intended our lives to be more than mere existence. We were made for a purpose, and God wants to see us restored to having right relationships with Him so that we can enter into the fullness of life. Satan, the enemy of our souls, wants us to look at our mistakes and give up. God wants us to see Him and look up. Jesus is the way, the truth and the life (see John 14:6).

PRAYER

Help me, Lord, never to forget that You made me for a purpose. I pray You will show me how to start living life to the fullest and discovering my true potential in God. In Jesus' name, Amen.

MY PLACE IN GOD'S WORLD

We will now turn our attention to the personal place God has for us in the incredible universe He created.

The Next Step on the Journey

When I take our dog for a walk on a dark night and look up at the painted ceiling of stars above my head, I understand what the psalmist must have been feeling when he saw the same stars and said, "What is man that you are mindful of him, and the son of man that you care for him?" (Psalm 8:4 ESV). He could not wrap his head around the fact that the God who made all the created realms claimed to know and love him personally.

The universe itself is so vast that it is beyond measure. That is not only a statement of Scripture (see Job 11:7) but also a scientific fact. As soon as man finds a way of measuring the distance to the farthest known heavenly body, astronomers discover a new way of detecting the existence of things even farther out. The edge of the universe does not seem to exist. It is without limit. You cannot measure the size of something that has no limits or boundaries.

It is hard for us to believe or understand that the Creator of this immeasurable universe could care about the individual life of any one human being. Or that the prayers of any one individual could be heard by a God who has over six billion children currently on planet earth.

Yet Scripture tells us that not even one sparrow falls to the ground without our heavenly Father knowing (see Matthew 10:29). Jesus urges us in verse 31 to remember that we are worth more than many sparrows.

If something you own is very valuable, you look after it, you protect it and you insure it. But all of your treasured possessions count as nothing when compared to the value of the life of someone you really love.

If your house was burning and someone you loved was still inside, you would not even think about rescuing the furniture. You would care far more about the person than any of your possessions.

Why Do You Feel Like That?

The reason we care about the people we love is that God created us to be like Him. He cares about the people He loves (see 1 Peter 5:7). He did not create a race of alien creatures with whom He has nothing in common.

Genesis 1:26 says that we are made in His image and in His likeness. Human beings are a reflection of the appearance of God—His image. To put it another way, the Son of God (Jesus) looked like a man and He was the image of His Father.

We are also made in His likeness. This element of humans is reflected in their natures. Scripture tells us that God is love. If, therefore, we are made to be like God, it must also mean that a capacity to love will be found in the heart of every human being, irrespective of whether or not they choose to believe in Him or love Him back.

That is why all unbelievers are still capable of great acts of personal sacrifice. It is also why unbelieving parents are still passionate about loving their children. People may behave very badly or do evil things, but you cannot totally eliminate love or the capacity to respond to love from the hearts of people.

I visited recently the home in which I was brought up as a child right after World War II. Times were hard, and my parents had very little to live on. But as I walked around that house, I was reminded of hundreds of things that my mom and dad did for me—often very sacrificially—because they loved me.

Because They Loved

Because my parents loved me, they cared for me. That meant they wanted what was best for me as I grew up, and they wanted to help me find my place in the world. They were thoughtful about encouraging me in the things I enjoyed. They saw the things I wanted to do or was good at and then tried to help me learn about those things and get better at them.

My mother would play the piano for a boys' Bible class that was held in our house. Before I was even five years old, I would sit at the piano and try to copy her; however, I could only make a joyful noise. I wanted to be able to play as she did, but I needed training.

At considerable personal sacrifice for them, they paid for me to have piano lessons from Miss Duxbury, an elderly lady with a very kind heart. I learned enough to enjoy playing hymns and choruses. As I grew, I developed a lifelong interest in Christian music. This led to me compiling hymnals and songbooks, such as *Mission Praise* (HarperCollins, 2015). I could not have done such things as an adult if I had not had their love and care for me as a child.

I realize that not everyone experienced the same love and care that I was privileged to have. For many people, their early childhood days were far from happy. But the good news is that God understands exactly what our experiences have been, and He longs to heal and restore us.

I know that many people throughout this journey are going to enter into a living experience of God's love and care, and as they do they will discover God to be their healer. I have seen it happen many times, and I know God can do this for you, too.

God Has a Place for You

Every human being is different. We are all made in the image and likeness of God, but our gifts, interests, abilities and opportunities are all totally different and utterly unique. Earlier we used the illustration of a jigsaw puzzle. Every single piece is different, but when all the pieces are in their proper places, a complete picture is made.

Each of us is like a unique piece in God's jigsaw puzzle. In His providence, He has equipped each of us for life, and He rejoices when we find the places that He has prepared for us.

Sadly, many people have never had the loving care from human beings that would have helped them discover the best places for them in God's world. Others have been hindered by their own ungodly choices or the awful consequences of violence, war, famine, accident, trauma or tragedy.

Does that mean God does not love them? Far from it. If you have a child who is hurting, you will pour all the love you can into that hurting child to bring hope, healing and restoration. We are like God in that respect. If a human parent would want to respond like that, imagine how much more Father God would respond in a similar way to all of His children (see Matthew 7:9–11; Luke 11:11–13).

Many times I have ministered to older people who were not given opportunities in their youth to discover their creative giftings. I have seen God heal their pasts and restore them in the present through discovering the joy of creative expression. The doors of their destinies have been unlocked by love.

Healed for a Purpose

These teachings have been planned deliberately as a journey and not simply as an aid in gaining more head knowledge. It is a journey of discovery—to discover the truth about both God and you and then to walk forward into God's plans and purposes for your life.

Healing is far more than recovering from physical sickness. It is seeing God restore what has been damaged in the past in such a way that we are able to experience God's fulfillment for our lives in the present. That experience then enables us to walk into the future that He has for us (see Jeremiah 29:11).

God created you for a relationship with Him, but He also created you to enjoy living in the purposes that He prepared for you in advance—His providence (see Ephesians 2:10). When we are being the people God made us to be and doing the things God made us to do, the joy of the Lord is released through our hearts. Life cannot be boring when you are at the center of God's will.

Over the years we have helped many people face the reality of their pasts and have seen God bring amazing healing into their present lives. But the greatest joy has come when we have seen those people begin to grow in their giftings and find the unique places that God has prepared for them.

I love that wonderful promise from Joel 2:25 where God declares, "I will repay you for the years the locusts have eaten." The locust devours, but God promises to give back in abundance when we have a right heart before Him. I pray that you will come to experience the blessing of this amazing promise as you journey through the pages of this book. You can trust the God who loves you so much that He made the whole universe for you to enjoy.

SUMMARY

God loves you and cares about you. Jesus promised that when He went back to heaven, He would prepare a place for us (see John 14:3). He also wants us to discover the place He has for us here as we respond to His loving care and receive His healing.

PRAYER

Help me, Lord, to lift up my eyes and not only see the extraordinary wonders of Your creation, but also realize that You care for every single human being—even me. Thank You for the miracle of Your love. In Jesus' name, Amen.

MY DESTINY IN GOD'S HANDS

We all need to know God's purposes for our lives. It is as we walk in the individual purposes that God has for each one of our lives that we begin to fulfil our personal destiny.

Men and Women of Destiny

I really enjoy reading the stories of great Christian pioneers and leaders. I especially like reading about people who believed for the impossible and obeyed God when they could have listened to the doubts of men and done nothing.

In the eighteenth century, William Carey went to India and translated Scripture into many different languages. In the nineteenth century, Hudson Taylor founded China Inland Mission and took the Gospel into mainland China. Charles Cowman founded the Oriental Missionary Society and opened up an amazing work in Japan before the first world war. And in the twentieth century, Jackie Pullinger took the Gospel and ministered healing to the drug addicts of Hong Kong.

There are many, many others. Some are famous, but the majority are unknown. Either way, they are very precious saints who did amazing exploits in obedience to God's call on their lives.

Reading their stories will encourage and strengthen you in your own Christian pilgrimage. They are stories of ordinary men and women who discovered their destinies and became agents of change for the Kingdom of God. They were envisioned by God, they responded with an uncompromising yes and history records the testimony of their achievements.

But What about Me?

I can hear some of you saying that the stories of such famous people are wonderful, but you could never do what they did. That is both a true and a false statement.

God never calls any of us to do exactly the same things as anyone else because every single one of us is totally unique. We have different looks, different gifts, different abilities and different destinies.

But it is completely false for you to think that you could not apply the same Kingdom principles in your own life and fulfill your destiny in God. You can. I have prayed that as we make this amazing journey together, you will see the fruit of doing that in your own life. You have the potential to do great things in the Kingdom of God as you enter into the destiny that He has prepared for you.

But do not worry about becoming great in man's eyes. It is only God's measure of greatness that matters (see Galatians 1:10). You do not have to become a famous pioneering Christian or have your name up in lights at some big meeting to be considered great in the Kingdom of God. All you have to do is be obedient to the vision God gives you—however large or small that is (see Proverbs 29:18; John 14:21).

My guess is that when the books are opened in heaven (see Revelation 20:12) there will be many, many people who were totally unknown on earth who will be considered great in heaven because of their simple faith and steadfast obedience (see Hebrews 11).

What Actually Is Destiny?

Sometimes people will come up to me at the end of a meeting and say something like this: "I would like some of your anointing. Will you pray for me?"

I understand the desire of their hearts, but generally I respond, "I can't actually pray like that, because you can't live my life, and I can't live yours. But I'd be glad to pray that God will give you His anointing for your life."

Anointing and destiny are linked closely, but they are not the same as gifting. It was the shepherd boy David's destiny to be the next king of Israel after Saul. He needed many gifts to fulfill the task. No doubt there were many other people in Israel who had similar gifts, but it was only David who had the destiny calling of kingship.

As soon as the Lord confirmed to Samuel that it was David who would be the next king, he took a horn of oil that was specially prepared, and he poured it over David. From that day on the Spirit of God rested on David (see 1 Samuel 16:13).

David was being prepared for his destiny. He had been anointed for the particular task (his destiny) for which God had prepared him. And the primary anointing David needed was the specific anointing that was relevant to his future role as king.

Finding My Destiny

The need to both be valued for who we are and to have a purpose in life is fundamental to every human being. Life without a purpose is meaningless. We all need a destiny to walk in.

I invited Jesus into my life at the age of nine. It was the best decision I ever made. At that moment, I knew for certain that my eternal destination had changed—heaven was now to be my future home. But I also knew that my earthly life would now have a purpose that was unique to me.

I began to pray for God to show me what He wanted me to do. While there were lots of things I was interested in, I was always thinking about some form of Christian ministry. My destiny was rising to the surface of my life. Without fully realizing what was happening, I was beginning to understand what God had planted deep into my spirit even before I was born.

This was Jeremiah's experience and testimony, and this is what God said about him: "Before I formed you in the womb I knew you, and before you were born I consecrated you; I appointed you a prophet to the nations" (Jeremiah 1:5 ESV).

As Jeremiah matured into a man of God, he connected with what God had already spoken into his being. He was discovering what God had made him for. He was discovering his destiny.

The picture on the front of a packet of seeds is never of the seeds in the packet. It is always of the plant in full bloom. The destiny of each seed in the packet is shown on the picture.

It is a bit like that with God—He sees our destinies on the packets that contain the seeds of our lives. As we grow in Him and mature as disciples of Jesus, we become aware of what He has in store for us.

Psalm 139:13 tells us how God created our innermost being and knit us together in our mothers' wombs. It is not only Jeremiah who had a destiny. God has had His hand upon us since those very earliest of days. He has longed to see us, His children, take the place in life for which He has prepared and equipped us (see Ephesians 1:4–5; 1 Corinthians 2:7–9).

Later we will see how Satan tries to rob you of your destiny and prevent you from fulfilling your calling in God. But we will also learn how to overcome the enemy.

God's Strategy for Your Destiny

God's fundamental desire for you is that you should find your eternal destiny in a restored relationship with Him. He wants to see you walk in your earthly destiny as a citizen of the Kingdom of heaven.

I was brought up hearing stories of two young women who were named Phoebe Lewsey and Ida Whittle. They both loved the Lord and sensed His call on their lives to bring hope and healing to children with leprosy in northern Nigeria. They sailed to Nigeria in faith and established the work of the Albarka Fellowship in Kaduna.

They were unknown to most of the Christian world, but in their faithfulness to the vision God had given them they experienced extraordinary protection and provision and saved the lives of hundreds of children. Ida personally experienced a miraculous healing from advanced cancer.

One day there will be a roll call in heaven of the lives that were transformed by the power of God through their ministry. They were living in their destiny. Today many of those children (and their children) are now serving the Lord in different parts of the world.

Scripture tells us that without vision people perish (see Proverbs 29:18). Vision brings life, hope, purpose and the fulfillment of destiny—both to us and to everyone whose lives are touched by ours. It is important, therefore, that believers look to God to give them vision for their lives. When we are living and serving Him within the visions that He gives us, we will know the greatest joy possible.

As unique individuals, God calls us to unique destinies. While some are called to the big things, others are called to smaller tasks. When the roll call of heaven takes place, God will not be looking for those who have achieved big things, but rather for those who were obedient to whatever was asked of them.

It Is Never Too Late for You

You may be thinking that because the early days of your life were a long way from ideal or that you really made mistakes along life's journey that you no longer have a destiny that can be realized. If you believe that God can no longer use you, you are believing a lie.

This is what Satan wants you to believe, for he is a destiny robber. His strategy is to interfere in your life to the point that you never realize the potential God has stored up for you. The good news is that Jesus overcame Satan at the cross. With Jesus as your helper there is an answer to even the very worst of situations. Later we will discover God's answers for the issues that may be holding you back in your life.

You will not be able to start life again at a young age, but God is the great Redeemer. Not only did He redeem you from the consequences of your sins, but He redeemed your life from the pit. He is the one who can restore the years that the locusts have eaten. He is the one who can take the humble offering of your life at whatever stage that you come to the point of absolute surrender and build something precious that will last throughout eternity.

All God asks of you is your availability and your obedience. He will then take whatever abilities you have and multiply them for His service.

I pray that as you walk this exciting journey, God will clearly show you His best for the rest of your life. And then, as you walk in obedience to His vision, He will give you the joy of being fulfilled in the service of the King.

SUMMARY

God not only loves and cares for each one of us, He also has a purpose for each one of our lives. When we are living the lives that He planned for us and His purposes are being fulfilled through us, we will know His joy flooding our hearts. We are children of destiny.

PRAYER

Help me, Lord, to discover the plans and purposes that You have for my life using the gifts and abilities You have given me. I want to discover my destiny and fulfill the vision You have for me. In Jesus' name, Amen.

MY SECURITY IN GOD'S LOVE

Each step of our journey together will put something more of God's amazing truth into your understanding. Or to use the illustration that we began with, into your God-box. The more truth there is in your God-box, the better equipped you will be for fulfilling the destiny that God has for you.

So far, we have established that our lives are precious to God and that what we do with them really matters—both to us and to Him. We know that God created the world for His people, and He rejoices when we find our place in it and discover our destinies.

We are turning our attention now to the deep inner need we all have for security.

The World as It Is

We are living in a world that is increasingly insecure, particularly for children.

Security and love are bound inextricably together. The break-up of many families and the consequential absence of fathering has removed much of the security that God desired children to enjoy within the safety and covering of families. As a result, we are now raising generations of children who have no secure family anchor. They are having to fend for themselves emotionally and physically, and they are being forced to learn how to be independent far earlier than God ever intended.

For those with no biological family around them, the familial relationships provided within the Body of Christ are to create that security and love. And yet the Body of Christ is not immune to the same threats that would remove those bonds. People are being orphaned spiritually by the effects of sin, and they are being forced to behave as if they are grown up long before they are ready to take on the responsibilities of adulthood. Even in the Church, relationships and the security they provide are under attack.

Sadly, the word *adult* no longer means simply a mature man or woman; rather, it is a description of the type of content people are looking at, specifically pornography.

We have fallen a long way from God's ideal, but this is the world in its current condition. Some of you may have been affected by these very issues. I am not drawing your attention to them just because I feel strongly about what is happening in the world, but rather because the Gospel has to be made relevant to real people in the real world. God has an intense interest in today's generations—from the young to the old and everyone in between.

Real Answers for Real Problems

The issues of life leave behind a legacy in the heart. Unless we have answers that will satisfy the deepest longings of the human heart, the Gospel is not good news for all but for only a chosen few. Those deepest longings usually lie hidden beneath the external behavior of those who are hurting.

People are hurting because of what has happened to them in the past. You may be one of them, wondering what God can do for people who have experienced neglect, trauma or the other results of less-than-perfect parenting. I want to assure you that there is no situation too bad that God cannot heal it, and there is no person so damaged that God is not concerned for them.

I believe passionately that the Gospel is good news for all. It is good for you, for me and for everyone to whom we are led. All are loved by our Creator. I pray you will want to share this good news with as many as are open to receive it.

But if we are to share it with others, we must first be willing to receive it for ourselves. We must allow Him to work it into our lives so that, as Paul prayed and longed for, we will grow up into maturity in Christ Jesus (see Ephesians 4:13).

JOURNEY TO FREEDOM is not only a training course to help you understand the truth of God's Word, but it is a dynamic experience of learning how to apply those wonderful truths. The application should happen first in your own life and then, following in the steps of Jesus, as a servant to others.

What Happens When We No Longer Know the Security of Love?

Security is a fruit of love. Without love there can only be insecurity, and insecurity breeds fear. It is no surprise, therefore, that Scripture tells us that perfect love drives out fear (see 1 John 4:18). We know that we can begin to trust and depend on Him in every area of our lives when we understand His perfect and completely selfless love (see Ephesians 3:16–19). Because we can trust Him, there is nothing to be afraid of. We are liberated from the bondage of our pasts into the freedom that is the inheritance of God's children (see Romans 8:14–17).

Fear, however, promotes independence and the need to control one's circumstances and environment. Independence makes people put up walls of self-defense. A need to control causes us to limit our life experiences to those we can be in charge of.

For many, the need for self-defense forces them to retreat into artificial fantasy worlds where they are in charge or where they find some comfort. Sadly, it is only false comfort and does not last. These false worlds can comprise anything from movie addiction to religion. They can range from dependence on music, computer games, other addictions (food, pornography or sex) or anything that can form a seemingly secure distraction from the realities of life.

Immorality has become the norm for the growing generations, not because they particularly want to be immoral, but because they do not know anything different. Parents and governments no longer have any moral boundaries of their own.

The presence of respect for God provides security through putting in firm and healthy boundaries for the next generation (see Proverbs 22:6; Ephesians 6:4). When there is no longer any respect or holy fear of God, there is no spiritual motive for disciplined love.

The old saying is very true—*the hand that rocks the cradle will one day change the world*. But if the hands that are rocking the cradle no longer know God, have no respect for Him and cannot understand how to really love their offspring, then we as a society are running quickly out of time to have an effect on the next generation to help them positively change the world.

Is There Any Hope?

This is a good question. It would be easy to look at all the bad things and decide to give up on wanting to make a difference for the Kingdom of God. Let me give you an example of what can happen.

The eighteenth century was a very violent and rebellious era in England. In spite of all the bad things one could point to, hope for the nation came in the form of a man with a message, John Wesley.

He was one of the greatest evangelists the United Kingdom has ever known. In the eighteenth century he changed the face of society through his determined preaching and Holy Spirit anointing. His preaching and passion turned the face of the nation away from violence and rebellion and laid the foundation for many of the good things that developed in the Victorian era of the nineteenth century.

His mother, the hand that rocked his cradle, was a woman of extraordinary godliness and passion who prayed individually with each of her fourteen children every day. She trusted that they would grow up to love and serve the Lord. They did.

John never forgot the influence of his mother on his life, and there are countless millions in eternity who will one day give thanks to God for John Wesley's mother. Even Hudson Taylor, the extraordinary founder of China Inland Mission, will be one of them. He was a second-generation fruit of Wesley's life and preaching. His life was used by God to transform the lives of many others. There is no one beyond hope.

Over the past 35 years, I have been privileged to see how God can transform the lives of even the most hurting people, many of whom did not know the love and security of loving parents but still came to know a loving God. He sent His agents to minister salvation and healing into their lives. Some of those people who received help are now some of the most whole people I know. God has healed them through love, has given them back the years that the locusts have eaten (see Joel 2:25) and has equipped them with a heart of love for others.

I am writing this because I want the whole Body of Christ to know these wonderful truths, to be empowered by the Spirit of God to take this message to His Church and to take that message into the world in which they live. I want people to regain an understanding of the security that comes through love. I want them to understand that hope and healing flow from the cross to all who will come to Him.

There is hope. Will you join with me in being willing to let the God of truth change you so that the truth of God can change others?

Security That Is a Fruit of Love

Security is both a feeling and a factual reality. In children the feeling of security is an emotional response to being loved by those who are responsible for them. Their physical security is the protection that is put in place by those who have the responsibility to love and care for them.

Our eternal security as a child of God is guaranteed by the love of our heavenly Father. John expressed it perfectly in one of the most well-known verses in the Bible when he said, "For God so loved the world that he gave his one and only Son, that whoever believes in him shall not perish, but have eternal life" (John 3:16). The sacrifice of Jesus was the ultimate demonstration of love. It was also the ultimate guarantee of eternal security. What an amazing promise those words contain.

But if you are one of those people who is living in the aftermath of rejection, betrayal, abuse, disloyalty or other painful experiences of childhood, do not fall into the trap of thinking that because your upbringing was hurtful that you will always suffer. That is a lie from the pit of hell. As we journey together you will see how the Lord can heal and restore you from whatever mess the enemy has made in your life and how He can give you the security of His love. You will find it helpful to read of God's heart to heal in Isaiah 61 and Psalm 91.

Yes, we do live in a fallen world. Yes, Satan is for the time being the god of this world, and yes, life can be tough as a result. Jesus, however, reminds us that "I have overcome the world" (John 16:33).

What truth. What promises. And what a Savior!

The Onward Journey

Next, we will be looking in greater depth at some of the vital foundations that must be in place in our lives in order for us to be strong in Him.

I am truly looking forward to hearing what He is going to do in and through you in the years to come as a result of our traveling together on this exciting journey.

SUMMARY

Security is a fruit of love. When we are loved we feel safe. When we truly know the heart of God and have experienced His love, then there is no limit to what God can do in and through our lives.

PRAYER

Thank You, Lord, for Your great love. I want to know the security that comes from knowing You. Help me, Lord, to forgive those who were responsible for all of the insecurity in my own life. Help me to grow in the knowledge and understanding of Your love so that there will be no barrier to me fulfilling Your destiny for my life. In Jesus' name, Amen.

STAGE 2

VITAL FOUNDATIONS

Poor foundations make buildings unsafe. Poor spiritual foundations make real life impossible.

ETERNITY IN THE HEART OF MAN

The foundation of a big building is never visible, but unless it is there, the building will collapse. We are now looking at the need for solid spiritual foundations relating to your knowledge of God and the life He has given to you.

Testing Days

The days in which we are living are very exciting and very challenging. World events are moving so fast it is hard to know where to focus one's attention. And in many parts of the world it is getting harder to be a Christian. Even in western nations, having a personal faith in Jesus Christ is ridiculed at every level of society.

A British TV presenter spoke recently of how difficult it was for him as a Christian to even mention his faith in the work environment. It was okay to talk about anything else—but not his Christian faith. You might live in a country that is even much more hostile to the truth of Jesus than this, or you may have experienced a more aggressive form of ridicule.

A major advertising campaign in the UK was funded by atheists. They put 800 advertisements on the sides of many of the buses. The slogan said, in very large letters: "There is probably no God." It was followed by words that encouraged you to go out and enjoy yourself without fear of God's judgment. Atheist interest groups in other countries also developed similar campaigns.

The assumption behind the campaign was that the very idea of God offends the intellect and restricts the enjoyment of life. It is assumed that anyone who believes in God cannot enjoy themselves.

Eternity in the Heart

The strange thing is that the creative gifting that dreamed up this campaign against God and Christianity came from God in the first place. This is how the writer of Ecclesiastes summed it up: "He has also set eternity in the human heart; yet no one can fathom what God has done from beginning to end" (Ecclesiastes 3:11). Men who profess to be clever are not clever enough to recognize from where their abilities come.

In the book of Job, we read a similar thought: "But it is the spirit in a person, the breath of the Almighty, that gives them understanding" (Job 32:8). Without the breath of the Almighty, man could have no understanding about anything.

The creative process, the ability to think and develop ideas or products, and the artistic genius that creates a great painting or a wonderful book all come from the Almighty. Without God, even atheists would not be able to do anything.

Because it is the Spirit of God that gives life to man (see Genesis 2:7; Acts 17:28) and it is the breath of the Almighty that gives him understanding, there is a deep recognition of eternal things in the heart of every human being—for God Himself is eternal. He has no beginning or end. The timelessness of eternal existence is part of our makeup, and it prompts people to believe that we must have come from somewhere, that there must be an afterlife and that death cannot be the end.

Death Is Not the End

If there were nothing of the eternal God in the heart of man, then there would be no reason for anyone to fear or be concerned about what follows death. People may not relish the process of dying or want to leave everything and everyone behind, but if there were nothing on the other side of death, eternal destiny would not be an issue.

I was once on a plane that filled with smoke. The effect was instantaneous—people began to cry out to God and pray.

When a U.S. Airways plane plunged into the Hudson River near New York City, it was reported that the passengers, every one of whom was rescued miraculously from the icy waters, began to cry out in prayer. There is only one reason for this. They were facing the prospect of premature death and an earlier than expected appointment with their Maker. That element of eternity in their hearts reminded people immediately that there is a God.

When faced with the possible sudden termination of life, man's instantaneous reaction is to respond to the breath of God within us. Perhaps it is because the spirit returns to its Maker at the time of death (see Ecclesiastes 12:7). At that moment people are aware of God from whom their spirits came and to whom they could be about to return.

The Evidence of God in the Children of Men

If something of the eternal nature of God is present in every human being, then we should expect to see some evidence of His character present in the human race. It is in Jesus that we have the one and only complete demonstration of the true nature and character of the God who made us all (see John 14:8–11).

We will be looking much closer at the life and ministry of Jesus later, but for now let us focus on two things that were preeminent in His life—*love* and *sacrifice*. Is there any evidence that love and sacrifice are present in humanity as a whole and not only in the lives of believers? Love and sacrifice are closely interrelated and yet are very different from each other.

When you see a young couple looking into each other's eyes, you do not need anyone to tell you they have fallen in love with each other. Love pours out of their every expression of word, affection and touch. They do not have to be believers to know the reality of love. When people love each other this way, they are willing to sacrifice all sorts of things as expressions of their love for each other.

When a mother cradles her newborn baby in her arms for the first time and she looks down at this precious bundle of life, she does not have to be a believer to be overwhelmed with love for this fruit of her womb. And when her child has a need and the mother only has enough resources to meet either the need of the baby or her own wants, it is a joy for her to sacrifice her own desires so that her child will not go without.

There are many more examples I could give, but the bottom line is that eternity (the very nature of God) is in the heart of man. It is the presence of God in man that makes him want to seek after God.

The Search for God

The search for God has been an ever-present reality for the human race since the very beginning of man's existence on the earth. Every people group that has been researched by anthropologists has been found to have developed their own religious beliefs and religious practices in an attempt to find God for themselves.

Amazingly, there are now well over three thousand identifiable religions. They all believe and practice something different from each other. The only factor common to all religions is that, while they are all different from each other, they all claim to be true.

It is extraordinary to me that in an attempt to bring peace and harmony, organizations such as the United Nations support the beliefs behind all of the world's religions as if they were all true. In reality, each religion is saying very different things, many of which contradict each other. The obvious fact is that either one is true and all the others are wrong, or all are wrong. But they cannot all be right.

Ever since man cut himself off from fellowship with his Creator in the Garden of Eden, he has been searching for an answer to the reason for his existence. In the heart of every human being is a huge question mark put there by God to both encourage an awareness of His existence and to cause man to seek after Him.

All of the other religions are versions of man's attempt to discover God. The fundamental difference between the Judaeo-Christian faith and all other religions is that Christianity is the story of *God seeking man*, not the other way around. Additionally, in all other religions, works of human effort are required in order to earn acceptance by their god. The only true God accepts and loves us from the outset and nothing we do can change His intrinsic love for us (see Romans 8:38–39).

Onward Christian Soldiers

Throughout our journey together, we will be discovering what God has revealed to us about Himself, about this world and about how we can enjoy fellowship and relationship with Him. He is the only One who understands who we are. He longs for us to know the depth of His sacrificial love for us so that we can enter into all that He has planned and purposed for our lives.

There is a God in heaven who loves you deeply. Imagine what He is going to do in your life in the months to come.

SUMMARY

Eternity is in the heart of every human being. It is the very breath of God that gave each one of us life. God sought us out to enjoy fellowship with Him, and He longs for us to know Him.

PRAYER

Thank You that the desire in my heart for relationship with You was put there by You in the first place. I am amazed by Your love for humanity and long to know You better and better day by day. Help me to get these foundations firmly in place so that the building of my life will be strong for the rest of my days. In Jesus' name, Amen.

THE FATHER'S HEART FOR **YOU** AND **ME**

Having established together that something of the heart of God is in the heart of every man and woman, we are now moving on to look at a second vital foundation for secure living—knowing that God as the ultimate Father of the whole of the human race is the very best of fathers.

Let us begin with a question: What was God's original plan for the fathering (and mothering) of humanity?

Fathering—the Original Plan

The Fall of man placed a barrier between God and man that could not be bridged by man alone. Without the Fall, people would have been in full relational fellowship with Father God. They would have had a clear understanding of the nature and character of God as their Maker, the source of their lives and their heavenly Father.

Ideally when children were conceived and born, they would have been brought up by their parents under the spiritual covering of their human fathers and in the love and nurture of the Lord. As they grew, they would have received from their parents a perfect understanding of the loving nature and character of God (see Ephesians 6:4).

The character and behavior of their parents would have demonstrated to them the character and nature of God, and there would have been no loss of understanding from one generation to the next. All generations to the present day would still know and understand the loving nature of the Creator God (see Hosea 11:1, 3–4).

There would have been no evil on the earth to cause pain or distress. The children would have been secure completely in the love of their parents, because their parents, in turn, would have been secure in Father God's love.

Such security would have given great confidence to every generation of children as they enjoyed using and developing all the creative gifts God had given them. We would all have been amazed at the creative potential demonstrated by every human being—probably to a far greater extent than the amazing things that have been possible for fallen man.

The Parenting Principle

The principle I am establishing here is that God as our heavenly Father delegated the job of fathering to human parents one generation after another (see Psalm 127:3–5).

God did not give babies and very young children the capacity to question and discuss issues with their parents. It is vital for their wellbeing and growth that they receive and trust that whatever their parents tell them or model for them is good. All of their energy must be spent on the vital processes of growth. They will have plenty of time later to ask the questions and discuss the issues of life. For now, they need to receive and be content in the loving provision of their parents.

God trusted that each generation would represent Him faithfully. He made children to believe instinctively that whatever they learned from their parents was the truth. As children absorbed everything that loving parents gave them, they would be absorbing the wonderful truth about the nature and character of God.

Everything a child is given is received and absorbed by them as if it is good—and if it *is* good there is no problem. But what happens if what is given to a child is not good?

Fathering—the Reality

It would be wonderful if the Fall had not happened, but we cannot pretend that we are living in a perfect world. We are not. We cannot avoid the stark facts of life on planet earth. It is messy. Life is unfair and people suffer in all sorts of ways—especially during the vital growing years that influence all the years that are to come.

I am not only talking about children who experience the more obvious traumas of life that occur in war-torn or famine-struck places of the world. I am talking about normal life behind the closed doors of the houses on the street where you live. Maybe even behind your own door.

In some countries, for example, as many as fifty percent of children are brought up in single-parent homes—mainly families without fathers. Some are in families where the children might not even know which one of the men Mom sees is their father. You might be part of that growing community of people who were brought up in a fatherless society where the mothers have struggled to be both a father and a mother to their children. A smaller number have been brought up in a motherless environment.

Many other children, even those who have been brought up in homes with both parents present, have been hurt deeply by the mothers or fathers they did have. These parents may have been so preoccupied with business, sports, their own interests or even church that they had no real time to nurture their children. Children need active time to receive parental love. Tragically, some mothers and fathers are cruel to their own children and even abuse them.

Not only do these children grow up with a belief that fathers and mothers cannot be trusted, they are also in danger of growing up with the belief that God cannot be trusted. As we learned from the God-box illustration, God intended that children should learn about Him from the way their parents behave. But when the behavior of the parents is bad, it is like telling the children a lie about the nature of God. God, Himself, has been betrayed. Sadly, because of the Fall, even the very best of human parents still falls a long way from God's ideal.

Food that is poisoned will kill a child, and an inadequate diet that omits essential ingredients will leave a child physically stunted in various ways. But a child who is brought up without love is also deprived and will not know how to either give or receive love. He or she will grow up with a defensive fight-for-myself mentality that shuns the very essence of humanity that he or she was created to enjoy—relationship.

You have suffered if you have not begun life with the depth of relationship that God intended for you to have. You may not have been deprived of physical food, but you are more than simply a body. You also have a soul and a spirit. If these vital dimensions of your humanity are starved of essential emotional and spiritual nutrients, then you will not develop into a well-rounded adult who is able to cope easily with all of the normal ups and downs of life.

We have to face the truth about ourselves and then ask God: What can be done about it?

Looking at the reality of this can cause some people to be depressed. They might cry out, "What hope is there for me?" If that is you, then be encouraged. God's heart for you is huge, and I have been privileged many times to witness God bring deep restoration and healing to people whose foundations were very different from what He intended.

The whole of JOURNEY TO FREEDOM has been designed to give understanding and hope to all of God's people (see Isaiah 49:13–16) so that they can receive healing for themselves and know how to minister to others.

A Hope and a Future

When we look at the life of Jesus, we see Him behaving in the way that many of us would have loved our human fathers to have behaved: loving, compassionate, concerned and interested in others. Scripture tells us that one of the reasons He came was to show us what the Father is like (see John 14:9). When we look at Jesus we can see the desire of God to be the spiritual Father of His children.

When good parents see their child hurting, they will always bend down to attend to whatever the problem is. The way a human parent behaves is a reflection of the way God longs to bend down and bring His hope and healing into our pain and brokenness (see Hosea 11:3–4).

As we have already seen, the breath of God is in each one of us. In spite of the fallen nature of man, we all still have that divine spark motivating our lives (apart from those who have given themselves over completely to the ways of darkness). It is wonderful to know that He longs to heal us of any damage in our lives that has come as a result of our parents so that we can fully connect with Him as our Father (see Isaiah 61:1–3; Jeremiah 29:11).

And Finally

Anne had been abused terribly by her human father. The damage was very deep. She had built her own defenses around the pain, but she could not sustain life under such stress. She was taken into care by the authorities and had little prospect of ever again being able to live a normal life.

But God intervened, and she learned about the Father's love. Eventually she was able to forgive her human father. Little by little God put back all that had been stolen from her. Today she is no longer just a lady with a past—she is living in the good of God for today with a hope and a future. Be encouraged!

SUMMARY

God is the very best of fathers. He is for you and wants you to know Him as He really is, whatever your own experience of human fathering has been. He longs to see you restored in Him and fulfilling your personal destiny (see Psalm 10:14).

PRAYER

Thank You, Lord, that You are for me every step of the way. Please forgive me for ever allowing my own experience of human fathering to color my understanding of who You are. I choose to receive Your comfort and healing in my heart and trust You as my heavenly Father. In Jesus' name, Amen.

SIN—REBELLION THAT SEPARATES FROM GOD

Each part of this stage of *Building on the Rock* is a bit like a trailer for a good film. A trailer gives you an insight into what the film is all about and an idea of what is coming later. Today's "trailer" is focusing on the subject of sin.

When we study the Fall of man a little later, we will look more closely at this concept. Unless we really understand how and why humans fell from their original place of intimacy with God, we will never comprehend fully what Jesus did for us on the cross.

But for now we are going to begin by getting an overview of what sin is. Do not worry if you are left with some important questions unanswered at this stage. They will be answered later.

Today's Mess

We have already reminded ourselves of the Father's love for every human being—including you and me. Now we will start facing the reality of the mess we see all around us that has caused such suffering down the ages and has brought a measure of suffering in our lives.

While the practice of sin seems to be very popular with the vast majority of human beings (otherwise we would not all be experienced at committing it), the idea of calling our behavior sinful is not at all popular. It is not politically correct.

Sin is also very selfish. In fact, sin is all about me and my world and not caring about others. Love cares for others, but sin only cares for itself and destroys the one we think we are caring for.

As human beings, we dislike being told that some of the things we are doing are wrong—not according to an arbitrary standard put in place by the different governments of the world, but according to an absolute standard that is applied to the whole human race.

The Word *Sin*

The word *sin* is unpopular because it introduces the concept that there is a God in heaven who has laid down a line with one side marked *right* and the other side marked *wrong*.

People do not like to be reminded of either the existence of God or this fact. And they do not like to think they are being thought of as sinners.

One of our prevailing temptations is to be wise in our own eyes and create our own personal standards of what is right and wrong (see Proverbs 3:7). We then can be our own moral judges and determine whether or not we have lived up to our own standards, however high or low they may be. When that happens, we do not have to submit our behavior to anyone else, least of all God.

The result of such thinking is that each of us develops his or her own personal morality that is unique to his or her own way of thinking. There are no longer any absolute standards. This is even reflected in the varying moral standards of the world's different religions.

While there are some behavioral standards that are common to the various religions, in many cases one religion will say that a certain thing is wrong while another will say it is right. The concept of right and wrong can change according to one's beliefs. Sometimes people even change their religion so that they can feel more comfortable with their behavior. There are, for example, some religions that allow a man to have more than one wife. But in other religions this would be seriously wrong and would warrant excommunication.

This lack of harmony between religions only serves to show how vital it is that we regain an understanding of the true nature of God. We need to know what His intentions are for humanity and what the idea of right and wrong means. Man's ideas about God will always conflict with each other.

The Idea of a Man-Made God

Without knowing the true God, we will only ever have a set of man-originated ideas as guides for life. Each and every one of us will develop an image of God made according to our own desires. We will manufacture a god to suit our own circumstances.

How can a created being manufacture the God who has created them? How can the creature (you and me) create something that is our spiritual superior (see Isaiah 44:9–20)?

We need to truly fear the God who made us and learn to respect His ultimate authority. He does not change His character or requirements from one religion to another. He cannot be locked up in the confines of a man-made idol. He is above all those things.

When respect for the ultimate authority of Creator God disappears from the foundations of our lives (and also from the foundations of governments), mankind slides quickly down a very slippery and destructive slope.

Understanding Sin—Free Will

To understand sin, we first have to understand that we are made in the image and likeness of God (see Genesis 1:26). This means that we have a free will.

No Christian would dispute that God, as ultimate Creator, exercised His free will in both the creation of the universe and in the creation of mankind. That was His choice. He created us for the purpose of enjoying a relationship with us. While we are not equal with God, we can have a relationship with Him. To do that, we need to have the attributes that enable relationships to exist. The most important two attributes are free will and the ability to give and receive love.

You cannot have a true relationship with a robot. You can only program a robot to do what you want it to do. A robot is incapable of independent choice or of producing a response motivated by love. It can be programmed to do an extraordinarily wide range of activities, but the robot is only responding to circumstances and instructions in a preplanned manner according to the way it was made.

My computer is a good example of a sophisticated robot. It does exactly what I tell it to do. It does not have a free will to do what it wants. It does not write a poem and then ask me what I think about it, and I do not have a meaningful relationship with it. I use it, and it is a tremendously valuable tool. But that is it. It is a sophisticated tool.

You are very different. You have a will of your own and are capable of making independent choices about anything and everything—and this is what you do thousands of times every single day of your life. That is how you are made and what you were made to do. You can choose to do whatever you like—both good and bad.

If you choose to do something wrong, a hand from heaven does not forcibly correct your behavior. You are truly free.

Conscience and Free Will

Deep in the core of your spiritual being you have a conscience. The conscience is part of the eternal dimension that is in the heart of every human being. It came from the breath of God when He breathed life into us.

When you are tempted to do something that is contrary to the will and purpose of God for you, your conscience will remind you of the presence of God, and you will be faced with a choice—either to carry on with your original intentions or to stop and change the direction in which you are going. Your conscience does not override your free will. It gives your will the opportunity to come into line with God's best for your life (see Romans 2:14–15).

Brother Lawrence, one of the early saints of God, wrote a book called *The Practice of the Presence of God*. He realized that we can never escape God's presence, no matter how hard we try. We should, instead, practice having a constant awareness of His presence. We need to develop our conscience into becoming a responder that is finely tuned to His presence, His will and His loving care.

The Essence of Sin

The essence of sin is not determined primarily by what our actions are in the presence of other people, but by what our actions are when no other human being is present—when it is only us and God and we still choose to rebel against Him.

If we know someone else is watching, our desire to do something wrong is restrained. That is the reason roadside cameras are a deterrent for speeding motorists. Someone is watching. It may be through the lens of a camera, but they are watching nevertheless. Fear of what might happen if we drive too fast and have an accident can also act as a deterrent.

It is interesting that Scripture refers to the fear of the Lord as a deterrent from sinning (see Exodus 20:20). If we lose the fear of the Lord, then we are, indeed, in great danger. Fear of God is a powerful deterrent of sin. Without it, we have lost one of the strongest protections against sin that we have.

Sinful actions are always preceded by sinful thoughts. Every single thing we do begins as a thought in our heads. The essence of sin, therefore, is determined by how we think and what we choose to dwell on in our minds. For what we think we will then do.

No wonder Paul encouraged his readers to take every thought captive and make it obedient to Christ (see 2 Corinthians 10:5). We may think we are totally alone with our thoughts, but God knows what is going on in our hearts (see 1 Samuel 16:7).

The origin of sin is always in the core of our being and has its roots in the pride of life, the lust of the eyes and greed. It is controlled by the selfishness of the heart (see 1 John 2:15–17).

When we are tempted, we might weigh the supposed benefits of the sinful behavior against the possible consequences. In doing this, we can then deceive ourselves into wrong courses of action. We might conclude that the pleasure of the sin will exceed the cost. In reality, that is all that was happening in the Garden when Adam and Eve tasted the fruit on the tree.

In Hebrews 11:24–26 we read how, by faith, Moses chose to be mistreated along with the people of God rather than to enjoy the pleasures of sin for a season. On the contrary, King David chose the pleasures of sin (with Bathsheba), and the consequences were serious for them both. Psalm 51 expresses what went on in David's heart when his sin was exposed.

Ultimately, therefore, sin is using our free will to make choices that are contrary to the nature and will of God. In simple terms, sin is rebellion against the God who made us.

Equal and Opposite Truths

There are many truths we will discover about God that seem to be equal and opposite at the same time. God has given us a free will and we have total freedom; however, He has also given us boundaries. He wants us to exercise our free will within these boundaries. It is freedom within limitations.

Those limitations are not hard walls or high fences that cannot be crossed, for we can use our free will to cross them whenever we choose. But when we do so, it is as if we are sowing bad seed. The apostle Paul tells us that the crop that we harvest in our lives will look like the seed that we sowed (see Galatians 6:7–9). The greatest blessings are always realized by choosing to sow good seed and living within the boundaries of God.

I will never forget the man who asked me what hope there was for his son. He had come to me for help because he had committed adultery, but so had his father and grandfather before him. The crop looked like the seed that had been sown by the generations before him. There *was* hope for him and his son, but he had to choose God's way and receive

God's answer. Later we will see how God can set us free from the consequences of bad seed that has been sown in our lives.

The Force of Law

When we disobey the voice of God or break His commandments as expressed in the Word of God, we will always find that law comes into force.

It is a bit like being warned not to go near the edge of a cliff because it is dangerous, but you use your free will to ignore the warning (the commandment) and continue walking over the edge. When you step over the edge, I can guarantee that at that moment the law of gravity will come into play, and you will discover the consequences of disobeying the warning the hard way.

We all know that the physical universe is ruled by physical laws. We cannot change these laws no matter how hard we try. We cannot pass a law in the United Nations to adjust the force of gravity. It is unchangeable. We must live our lives within the confines of those laws. If we do not, we will die—sometimes very quickly.

In a similar way, we are also spiritual beings living in a spiritual universe, and there are equally unchangeable spiritual laws that are in force. If we choose to disobey the commandments of God, we will discover the spiritual laws that control the spiritual universe.

And that is exactly what mankind has done. We have disobeyed God's first commandment to Adam and discovered the consequences of spiritual laws the hard way. As a result of one man disobeying God's commandments, death entered into the whole human race (see Genesis 3). It is only in Jesus that there is a way of escape from the consequences of man's sinful choices (see Isaiah 53:3–6).

The Nature of Sin

The nature of sin, therefore, is much more profound than breaking rules that are put in place by one of the many world religions or governments. Sin is rebelling in one's heart against the fundamental nature and character of God and choosing not to walk in His ways.

The first commandment tells us not to have any other God than the God who made us (see Exodus 20:3). When man listened to the voice of the tempter, Satan, and obeyed him rather than God, a set of consequences was put in motion. Those consequences will continue to affect humanity until the day that God brings this current world to a close with the return of Jesus Christ. At the Fall, mankind came under Satan's control, and Satan became known as the god of this world.

Later we will look more carefully at who Satan is and how he gained such a controlling influence on planet earth. But for now all we need to understand is that the rebellion of our first parents left all of the sons and daughters of Adam living in a prison of man's own making that was controlled by the guilt and power of sin. Man broke the commandment (not to eat of the fruit of the Tree of Knowledge of Good and Evil) and the rest, as they say, is history. Man's history, your history and my history.

The Consequences of Rebellion

The consequence of man's rebellion (sin) for the human race was being cut off from the fullness of relationship with God (death). Since that time, man has not only had to contend with the temptations from without, such as what Adam and Eve faced, but also with the temptations from within.

We have all inherited the rebellious nature of the human heart. Even the apostle Paul had to wrestle with the temptations of his inner being (see Romans 7:14–25).

Physical death did not ensue immediately from the Fall of man, but spiritual death, the breaking of relationship with God, *was* immediate. Physical death was an eventual consequence. What God had warned Adam about certainly happened.

Next the Good News

We have now studied the bad news—but there is good news to come as we look at how God responded to what man had done in choosing to disobey Him. It is good news to which we can really look forward.

SUMMARY

Man has messed up by choosing to resist the loving will of Father God and to follow the deceptive lies of Satan. All of humanity is suffering as a result. But it is only by understanding what has happened that we can also understand what God planned to do about it.

PRAYER

I recognize that there is sin in my own heart. I want to make right choices and follow Your ways, Lord. Help me to understand what sin is and then to walk away from it for the rest of my days. In Jesus' name, Amen.

JESUS—SAVIOR AND FRIEND OF SINNERS

In the previous stage of our journey, we had to face the bad news about what sin has done to the human race. But it is now time for the good news—the especially good news of what the Savior has done for every one of us. As you read this, it may be the first time that you understand truly what Jesus did for you on the cross.

I have often seen that when people understand the depth of Jesus' sacrificial love for them, they are able to receive His healing love in their lives, and they want to walk in His ways.

Thinking through and writing this material has had a profound influence on me. Looking again at all that Jesus has done for me has both challenged and inspired me to keep running the race for the rest of my days.

In Prison

A friend of my father's went through the trauma of his son committing a crime and going to prison. After the son had served his time, my father offered to collect him from the prison gates and bring him home.

On the day he was to be released, I went with my father to the prison and waited outside the gate. At precisely 7:00 a.m. a door in the prison wall opened, and the young man came out. The prison was no longer his home. He was a free man.

I have never forgotten the dramatic moment when he turned his back on the prison walls for the last time. He had paid his debt to society and was now free again to live his life in whatever way he wished.

In days gone by there was another sort of prison in the city of London—a debtor's prison. It was a terrible place reserved for those who owed money but who, for whatever reason, were unable to pay their bills.

They could not serve their time and be released. There was only one way out of their stone-walled pit of human misery. They needed someone else to have compassion on them and pay the debt that was owed.

The famous English novelist Charles Dickens tells of how as a child he had to work to pay off his father's debts. His father was in the notorious Marshalsea Debtors' Prison, and his freedom could only be bought by someone else paying the debt. There was no other way out. In his novel *Little Dorrit*, Dickens drew on this awful time of his own life and built into the story his personal experience.

Man's Condition

Mankind is also in a prison. When we look more closely at what happened in the Fall of man, we see how man used his own free will to obey Satan rather than to obey God. The moment that happened, the special relationship man had with God was broken, and the gates of death closed behind the whole of the human race.

Jesus tells us clearly that hell had not been prepared for human beings (see Matthew 25:41) but for the devil (Satan) and all his angels. By obeying Satan and coming under his authority, man destined himself to be in the same place and condition as Satan for all time and eternity. Mankind had placed himself in a prison controlled by Satan. In doing so, Satan's destination had also become the destination of man.

It was as if man had chosen not only to enter a prison, but to also build the walls of his own prison. Walls that would keep him confined for the rest of time. Every member of the human race has been conceived and born within those same prison walls.

It was like a debtor's jail, because the people inside could only get out if someone else paid the price for their release. There was absolutely nothing they could do from inside the prison to either organize their escape or pay the price for their release.

Man's authority now belonged to Satan, and Satan used it to draw worship to himself and serve his own purposes. Mankind would have to live and die inside the debtor's jail.

Even though man had been created to enjoy eternal fellowship in heaven with God, mankind was now separated from God and under condemnation. He was in a debtor's jail, and he had lost his eternal destiny in heaven.

Motivated by Love

Scripture tells us that God is love (see 1 John 4:8). Love is the most powerful force in the world. Love was the power that created the universe. It was the desire of a loving God to create mankind for fellowship and relationship with Himself.

When a baby is born most parents adore and love their newborn child. He or she means everything to them. As far as they are concerned, their baby is perfect. Their love knows no limits.

But when the child starts to grow bigger, the time comes when their formerly perfect baby starts to misbehave. When that happens, the parents still do not stop loving their child. This is their precious offspring born of their flesh. Even though the child is being naughty, the parents have no desire to try to exchange their child for a different model. They may be saddened by bad behavior, but this is their child, and their love knows no limits.

Throughout life many parents will go to great lengths to show their love for their children—even in very extreme circumstances. I watched pictures of a mother leaving a jail having visited her son for the last time before his execution for murder. Even though he had done terrible things deserving of the death sentence, this was her boy. The tears of compassion poured freely down her face as she tried to tell people how much she loved him.

Where do parents get that sort of love? They get it from their Creator. We are made in the image and likeness of God, and even though man made mistakes with eternal consequences, God did not stop loving His children. The life of all of His children came from the very breath of God (see Genesis 2:7). He longed for the restoration of fellowship that had been stolen from Him soon after man's creation.

The jail that mankind was now in could only be opened by someone with higher authority than the jailer. While God has all power and all authority, He has given man authority over the earth; therefore, only a man who had never come under Satan's control could exercise that authority. Only a sinless man living on earth could provide mankind the possibility of stepping free from Satan's stronghold.

Death was man's inheritance, and the price of death had to be paid (see Romans 6:23). Since all sinners are born inside the jail, it could be paid only by a man who had never sinned, otherwise his death would be to no avail. Someone from outside the jail had to pay the price.

Born on Earth—but Outside the Jail

God's plan of salvation was worked out on the stage of planet earth. The babe of Bethlehem was conceived by the Holy Ghost in the womb of a virgin girl.

He was not born as a product of a normal human relationship. He did not, therefore, carry the stain of sin passed down from His earthly father. His inheritance was from God, not from Joseph. He was born outside the jail.

He resisted every temptation of the enemy and never came under Satan's control. When the final act of God's human drama was played out at Calvary, there was only one star on that most primitive of stages.

The soldiers drove in the nails, but it was love that held the Son of God to the cross. As He hung there, the destiny of every human being—past, future or present—hung in God's balance. Heaven must have held its breath as the Son of God breathed His last as a human being.

At that moment, the veil of the temple that separated man from the presence of God in the most holy of places was torn from top to bottom.

A way was reopened for mankind to once again have fellowship with the Father. This time it was through Jesus, the Son.

Sin had not broken the relationship between Father God and Jesus the Son. On resurrection morning there was a Man on earth who had the keys of heaven, death and hell in His hand. He had a higher authority than the jailer, Satan, and because of that, the price for the freedom of the prisoners was paid.

Death had been overcome, and there was a way that man could once again look forward to heaven's glory. The invitation to freedom rang out through all the rooms in the debtor's jail and down through all the ages of time.

Jesus had fulfilled the promise of all those wonderful Old Covenant prophecies. A perfect sacrifice had been made for the sins of the people. The New Covenant had come, and to all who chose to receive Him, He gave the right to be the children of God (see John 1:12). What joy, what release, what freedom—what a Savior!

New Birth

Those who receive the good news and accept the extraordinary gift of salvation that Jesus won for us all on the cross are given a new life outside of the prison walls. They are given a fresh start at whatever age they receive the gift. At that point they are born again.

They are released from the jail of the kingdom of darkness and have become citizens of a glorious Kingdom. It is the Kingdom in which Jesus, the Son of God, reigns as King.

The debt has been paid, and Satan is powerless to keep those who choose to believe in Jesus inside the debtor's jail. They have used their free will to accept God's answer. They are free for the rest of time and eternity beyond. They are born again to new life (see John 3:16).

The Tragedy of the Cross

The greatest tragedy of the whole history of the human race is that the god of this world (Satan) has blinded the eyes of humanity so completely that the majority of human beings choose to remain in the familiar surroundings of the debtor's jail even though there is now a way out (see 2 Corinthians 4:4).

Mankind still has a free will, but sadly most people use their free will to turn away from the joy of salvation. They prefer the paths of pride and pleasure, or they choose to stay chained by the demands of wrong religious beliefs. For many, what they believe they would have to surrender seems too costly, and they would rather live their lives their own way. But the door of hope is still open for all men and women who choose to respond to the love of the Savior.

It was love that motivated the heart of God to remain faithful to us even though we had sinned. Love is still the motivation for those of us who have received the gift of God to go into all the world and make disciples. That is the commission that Jesus gave to the Church (see Matthew 28:19).

And it is also what JOURNEY TO FREEDOM is all about—teaching people to be disciples of Jesus for the Kingdom of God and to proclaim faithfully the wonderful news of the Gospel all of their days.

Sheer Joy

It was the joy of victory and of man's salvation that was set before Him that gave Jesus the courage to push through the cross. He knew that He would experience the joy of being able to fellowship in heaven with you and with me (see Hebrews 12:2) and that He would be able to present to His Father those who had been redeemed out of the hand of the enemy.

The Gospel is not only good news, it is undeserved and sensationally good news. What grace, what mercy!

I once had a friend who resisted the truth about Jesus, but he said these words that I have never forgotten: "If I believed what you believe, I would be willing to crawl on my hands and knees across broken glass to tell every human being the Gospel of Jesus Christ."

God was merciful to this honest man. He wanted to know the truth, but he had been confused and disturbed by the myriad of different religions that all claimed to have the truth. He worked hard and was a loyal and trusted friend. But he took ill, and at the end of his life he lay in hospital dying.

I looked into his eyes and shared with him once again the sensational news of the Gospel. I do not know whether the Lord gave him a distant view of heaven's glory or if He revealed the Son of God's face to him in that moment, but something happened. The scales of unbelief fell suddenly from his eyes. I was able to grasp his hand as he invited Jesus to be his Lord and Savior.

I never saw him again on earth, but I know that one day I will see him in heaven. He escaped from the debtor's jail at the very last moment. As the Parable of the Workers in the Vineyard makes plain, the reward of salvation is the same for those who come to Him at the end of their lives as those who find Him at the beginning (see Matthew 20:1–16).

The love of Jesus surpasses everything. Jesus is truly both a wonderful Savior and a friend of sinners. He is my friend, and I trust He is yours. Put your hand in His, and He will be your companion through every day of the rest of your life. This good news has transformed my life. I pray it has transformed yours and that you will want to keep serving the Lord Jesus for the rest of your days.

SUMMARY

Jesus came from heaven's glory to show us how much the Father loves us. Jesus is the friend of sinners, and He gave His life to pay the price of freedom for all of humanity. But only those who accept the gift can claim their inheritance in heaven.

PRAYER

Thank You, Jesus, for being such a wonderful Savior. Thank You for Your amazing sacrifice on the cross. Thank You for forgiveness for my own sin. Thank You for being my Friend—in time and eternity. In Jesus' name, Amen.

HOLY SPIRIT— EMPOWERMENT FOR GOD'S PEOPLE

Jesus did extraordinary things in His relatively short life, and what He set in motion is still being experienced today. Even in His absence on earth, the Church has not only survived for two thousand years but it has also defied every attempt by the enemy to eliminate its believers and to destroy it. It is an incredible story. I wish we had more time to look together at the testimonies of some of the amazing saints down the ages who have kept the flame of truth burning brightly even when the darkness tried to extinguish it. People like:

- Stephen, the first Christian martyr, who was stoned to death (see Acts 7:54–60).
- Bishop Polycarp, who was burned at the stake for his extraordinary faith and trust in God.
- The bishops of the Church of England in Oxford, who also were burned at the stake because they were committed to putting the truth of God into the language of the common people.

- The Huguenots, who endured persecution in France because of their faithfulness to God.
- The young believers in Uganda, who suffered a terrible fate in the early days of the East African church.
- In more recent days, the countless believers in China, who paid the ultimate price for their faith and whose names are written in heaven.

I have reason to be thankful to God for the Huguenots because my own direct ancestor Jacob de Villiers was one of those determined believers who would not renounce his faith. He fled France on the good ship *Zion* to South Africa in 1680 with his brothers Abraham and Pierre. Many generations later I am still being blessed by the fruit of his faithfulness.

Where did all of these people and countless millions more throughout human history get the courage to remain faithful to their Savior? Was it the prospect of heaven for those who were born again? Or was there something more? Let us look at the Word of God together.

Power from on High

Scripture tells us that Jesus was conceived by the Holy Spirit, and He was led by the Holy Spirit all His life. But there was a critical moment in the earthly story of the Son of God when He went to be baptized by John the Baptist.

John's baptism was a baptism of repentance, but Jesus had never sinned. John knew that Jesus was the perfect Lamb of God who would take away the sins of the world. No wonder John could not understand why Jesus was in line waiting to be baptized in the River Jordan (see Matthew 3:1–17). John argued that Jesus should have been baptizing him, not the other way around.

But Jesus was adamant. It was necessary for Jesus to be baptized. This was the moment when Jesus associated Himself with sin, yours as well as mine, by allowing Himself to be baptized in a baptism of repentance.

Three years later He was to die for the sins of the world. But at this critical moment He stood in an act of repentance on behalf of all those who would believe in Him for the forgiveness of their sins. This was the moment above any other when Jesus accepted publicly His commission from Father God. It was the whole reason He came to earth.

When He came up out of the water, the joy in heaven could be contained no longer. The Father was thrilled at what He was seeing, for the great salvation plan was being fulfilled.

From heaven's glory the Holy Spirit of God was poured out in full measure upon Jesus. The people saw the Spirit descend upon Jesus in the form of a dove, and they heard the Father's voice say, "You are my beloved Son; with you I am pleased" (Luke 3:22 ESV).

Heaven approved. The first step was taken toward the eventual completion of the plan of salvation. Jesus was now full of the Spirit in a new way.

As a result, He was led by the Spirit into the wilderness to face the most severe temptations Satan could throw at Him. In a later study, we will see how Jesus resisted them all and came back from the wilderness not only full of the Spirit but now operating in the power of the Spirit (see Luke 4:1–14).

Seeking the Key

Many years ago, I was looking to God for direction regarding the fact that I was sensing His call on my life in the ministry of healing. I did not know how to respond to the call, so day by day I continued to pray into the vision. For many years, however, there was no apparent response.

One day I was in church crying out desperately to God, and I heard Him say, "Go home and read the Bible."

I was a little confused. The problem was that I did read the Bible most days and had done so since I was a young child. What did the Lord mean? As I walked home that night, He began to help me understand that He wanted me to read it more like any other book—straight through. He did not want me to only read a few verses here or a few verses there.

I started that night at the beginning of the New Testament and read all the way through Matthew and Mark's gospels. It was all very familiar. But when I got to the last chapter of Mark's gospel and read the words "They [believers] will place their hands on sick people, and they will get well" (Mark 16:18), I was electrified in my spirit. God was speaking to me.

I looked at my hands, and they still looked like very ordinary hands. I wondered what this verse really meant. I read on right through Luke's gospel, on into John's gospel and into the beginning of the Acts of the Apostles. Once again, I was stopped by God.

There in chapter 1 and verse 8 was the key I had been looking for: "You will receive power when the Holy Spirit comes on you." My hands without the Holy Spirit were just hands.

Through this verse God was speaking to my heart and was saying that the hands of any believer who is filled with the Spirit and who is doing what God has asked them to do will be filled with power.

Baptized in the Spirit

From that moment on I began to seek the baptism of the Holy Spirit. I had read various books about the work of the Spirit, but until I began to respond positively to the call of God upon my life, the experience of the Spirit in this New Testament manner as was described in the Acts of the Apostles on the Day of Pentecost was foreign to me. A few nights later, however, at 1:00 a.m. I was wide awake. Although I could not see any tongues of fire, I felt as though I were on fire and glowing from head to foot.

I had no idea what was happening until I heard the Lord's gentle voice say, *It is okay, it is only me.*

These were words that my parents used to say to me as a child when they returned to the house after I had been left alone. They were words of comfort and security. God was assuring me by using these very familiar words that the owner of the house (God) was in residence (in me). As Scripture teaches us, our body is the temple of the Holy Spirit (see 1 Corinthians 3:16, 6:19).

From that moment on, I was alert to the Spirit of God in a way that was totally new to me. I knew that without the Holy Spirit having drawn me to God in the first place, I could never have been born again. I also knew that it was the Holy Spirit who had brought Scripture to life for me. There was no doubt that in the past I had experienced the Spirit of God guiding me, directing me and even protecting me. But this was different.

I knew that God had heard and answered my prayer. Within a short time, I received the gift of tongues and was able to worship God in a new language. It may or may not have sounded like the tongues spoken by the disciples on the Day of Pentecost, but I was very aware of the presence of God. I had a new and determined desire to live out the vision God had given me for the healing ministry. In some ways it felt as though my Christian life had begun afresh.

Not everyone's experience of being baptized in the Spirit is the same. God deals with each one of us in unique ways. Some may have a very dramatic experience, while others may become aware of the reality of God's indwelling presence. Like conversion, everyone's experience is different. But it is important that you do know that you have been filled and are continuing to be filled with the Holy Spirit day by day. If you are not sure how to pray, you will find help below at the end of this stage of the journey.

The Fruit and the Gifts of the Spirit

Later we will look more closely at the gifts of the Holy Spirit. These are the supernatural abilities that come to every believer who is baptized in the Holy Spirit of God. But it is important to remember at this stage that the gifts and the fruit are not the same.

The fruit of the Spirit is the very nature of the God who is love. While the gifts of the Spirit are received in a moment, it can take a significant period of time to have been walking with the Lord for the characteristics of His loving presence to become evident in our lives and to change us from the inside out.

It is the fruit—joy, peace, kindness, etc. (see Galatians 5:22–23)—that flows from love and is the true hallmark of a life that is being lived in fellowship with God. We need the gifts to do the works of the Kingdom, but the fruit is the vital qualifying factor to be able to exercise the gifts. Without the fruit, any manifestation of gifts is out of order and is meaningless (see 1 Corinthians 13:1–3).

My Prayer for You

It is my prayer for you that your heart's desire will not only be to grow in the character of Jesus but to also receive the Spirit of God and the gifts of the Holy Spirit to help you live your Christian life. When Peter preached to the people at Pentecost he said:

> "Repent and be baptized, every one of you, in the name of Jesus Christ for the forgiveness of your sins. And you will receive the gift of the Holy Spirit. The promise is for you and your children and for all who are far off—for all whom the Lord our God will call."
>
> Acts 2:38–39

As we reach the end of stage two of our journey together, I would like to invite you to say a prayer with me. It is a simple prayer and may even be one that you have prayed before. I would like to invite you to make Jesus the Lord of every area of your life.

Within the work of Ellel Ministries, we meet many Christians who are well aware of their need for salvation and are looking forward to heaven when they die, but who still really struggle with making Jesus the Lord of their lives. Often the reason is that they remain unhealed and are not able to be baptized in the Holy Spirit.

In reality, Jesus is the key to everything, and making Him Lord is the most important thing you can do as you seek to live for Him while on earth. For thousands of people who have come for help at one of our Ellel centers, it has been the master key that has unlocked their healing and transformed their lives.

SUMMARY

The Holy Spirit was God's gift to Jesus and is also His gift to the Church. Without the Spirit, you cannot fulfill your destiny. With the Spirit, you grow more like Jesus day by day as you trust Him to change you from the inside out. You can also be empowered with the gifts of the Spirit to do the works of the Kingdom of God.

PRAYER

If you want Jesus to be Lord of every area of your life, say this prayer slowly, phrase by phrase, meaning it from your heart:

Thank You, Jesus, for dying on the cross for me. I confess that I am a sinner in need of a Savior. I choose to repent and turn from my sins. I invite You now to be Lord of every area of my life—Lord of my mind and all my thinking, my beliefs and my imagination; Lord of my emotions and all my reactions; Lord of my will and all my decisions; Lord of my body and all my behavior; Lord of my sexuality and its expression; Lord of my family and all my relationships; Lord of my work, my finances, my needs and my possessions; Lord of my spirit and my relationship with God. Thank You that Your blood was shed that I might be set free from the punishment due for my sin and that my name is written in the Book of Life. Come, Lord Jesus, and reign in my life for all of my days. Amen.

Then you can pray like this for God to fill you with His Spirit:

Thank you, Lord, for the promise of your Holy Spirit. Come and fill me to overflowing that Your Spirit will empower me day by day to live for You. In Jesus' name, Amen.

STAGE 3

THE BIBLE—MY GUIDE FOR LIFE

*Without a map, I get lost. Without the Bible,
I am lost before I even begin the journey.*

GOD'S AMAZING LETTER TO THE HUMAN RACE

We are now going to focus our attention on the importance of reading the Bible as our daily guide for Christian living. We will take a fresh look at how it can be a source of great blessing every day of our lives. We will see how God chose to reveal His plans and purposes in the Bible and how critical this amazing book is for each one of us.

We have already covered a significant amount of ground in our journey of discovery. It is a journey that will take us deep into the things of God and will equip us to live godly lives.

The most important decision any of us can ever make is to invite Jesus to be the Lord of every area of our lives. We will return to this subject on numerous occasions as we experience the personal transformation that He can bring.

It is only the presence of God that can change everything in our lives. In His presence we are motivated to become the people that He can make us to be. It is His presence that equips and empowers us to fulfill our destinies. The Bible talks about our steps being ordered by the Lord (see Proverbs 16:9). When He orders our daily steps through life, we can certainly trust the outcome.

There are many occasions when I have sensed the Lord ordering my steps. He has taken me in a particular direction or encouraged me to do a certain thing at a certain time. Time and time again, I have been amazed at the outcome. What a faithful God we serve.

On one occasion I sensed God telling me to drive to a certain place. It meant going out of my way, and I was already late. I had no idea why He was directing me this way, but I chose to obey what I thought He was saying. When I got to where He was directing me, I was amazed to see a familiar person. It was a lady we had been helping who needed to overcome some deep issues. She could not believe that I had turned up at the critical moment. She was sitting by a deep lake and told me that she had come to this place to commit suicide. By listening to what God was saying to me, her life was saved.

But there have been occasions, too, when I knew that God was speaking to me, and I chose not to listen. On one particular occasion, I did not want to hear what God was saying because I knew it was the opposite of what I wanted to do. I made a wrong choice that very nearly cost me both my business and my life. Disobeying God is always costly.

His leading may sometimes take you in directions that in the moment might be surprising, but in retrospect it proves to be a source of great blessing. On some occasions His leading may help you to avoid unforeseen pitfalls. For me, the Lord's direction has often come through a particular word of Scripture.

The Bible Is a Love Letter from God

I remember striking up a friendship with a girl during my teenage years. We started writing letters to each other, so the daily delivery of mail became very exciting. When a letter did come, I would read it through multiple times. I did not want to put it down.

That is how you need to approach the Word of God. It is a love letter from God Himself. It is a letter to the human race from the most loving Father there has ever been. If you can learn to treasure what God has said in His Word and store it in your heart, then it will be the source of truth and guidance for all the days of your life. It will also be the very best defense you can ever have against deception and the inroads of the enemy.

If you can learn to receive from the Word of God every day and live it out in your daily life, I guarantee that the truth of God's Word will bring personal transformation. The ability of God's Word to bring transformation is at the heart of our journey to freedom.

It has been exciting to look at the wonderful gift of salvation that Jesus brought to us through His death and resurrection, and then to discover how the Holy Spirit is such a vital key to living the Christian life. This same Holy Spirit was the inspiration behind the most important book in the world. The Bible is a book that does not simply contain the Word of God, as some people say, but it *is* the Word of God to the human race.

Paul expressed it this way in 2 Timothy 3:16–17: "All Scripture is God-breathed and is useful for teaching, rebuking, correcting and training in righteousness, so that the servant of God may be thoroughly equipped for every good work." JOURNEY TO FREEDOM is all about us getting equipped thoroughly for every good work that God wants each one of us to do.

The World's Most Valuable Possession

Queen Elizabeth II of England has been on the throne for a very long time—longer than any other monarch in British history. Her father, King George VI, died when she was still quite young. I am old enough to remember that day in 1952. The whole nation went into mourning with the death of the much-loved king who had brought us safely through the dark days of war.

The queen's coronation as Her Majesty Queen Elizabeth II took place on June 2, 1953. Television was still in its infancy. Only a very small number of relatively wealthy people could afford such an amazing machine. To watch the coronation on television, our family went to the home of our local doctor in Northern England.

At least twenty people were crammed into a small room. We focused our attention on a tiny black-and-white screen that broadcasted the proceedings in Westminster Abbey in London. Even though I was only nine years of age, I was enthralled by what I saw.

It was a holy moment in the nation's history when, in the middle of the coronation service, the queen promised to maintain God's laws and the true profession of the Gospel.

When she said those words, the archbishop of Canterbury presented her with a Bible and said, "We present you with this Book, the most valuable thing that this world affords. Here is Wisdom; this is the royal Law; these are the lively Oracles of God."*

What an incredible statement. The most valuable thing in the world. Of more value than all of the world's riches. More important than any other book. It is a book that does not simply contain wisdom but actually *is* wisdom. The royal law that even kings and queens acknowledge has an authority greater and higher than theirs.

"The lively Oracles of God." This is an old usage of the word *lively*, and it simply means "living." The oracles of God are His revelations to humanity.

What a statement that describes this most amazing book that is the ultimate source of truth (see John 17:17). It is the source of knowledge about the One who described Himself as the truth (see John 14:6). Without the Bible, we would have no knowledge of God's extraordinary revelation of Himself to mankind.

Richard Wurmbrand, who survived fourteen years in a communist jail for his faith, put it this way, "The Bible [is] the only book capable of satisfying the spiritual needs of the world."†

Everything you will learn on our journey to freedom has its origin in the Bible. It is the most important book you will ever possess.

The Story of the Bible

Some people are excited by history while others find it boring. But whether you like it or not, history is important. Much of the Bible is a history book. It is not a dry or very boring catalogue of events, but rather it is a living record of the people who made history and of the lessons we can learn from their experiences.

---

*Simon Kershaw, "The Form and Order of Service that is to be performed and the Ceremonies that are to be observed in The Coronation of Her Majesty Queen Elizabeth II in the Abbey Church of St. Peter, Westminster, on Tuesday, the second day of June, 1953," Oremus, version 12, March 11, 2017, http://www.oremus.org/liturgy/coronation/cor1953b.html.

†Richard Wurmbrand, *Christ on the Jewish Road* (Middlebury, Ind.: Living Sacrifice Books, 1975), 9.

The Bible itself has a remarkable history, starting with the way the Jewish rabbis first gathered the ancient books and put them together in the Tanakh. The Tanakh contains the same books as our Old Testament, but they are arranged in a different order.

It took nearly 400 years for the early Church fathers to be in complete agreement about which books should form the New Testament Scripture.

Our Bible today contains 66 books and was written by over 40 different authors over about 1,500 years. While there may have been 40 human writers, there was only one ultimate author—the Holy Spirit. The Holy Spirit inspired all of the contributing writers.

Because the Bible is God's Word to the human race, the god of this world has done everything he can to oppose those who would want to make Bibles available to people in languages they understand. It is hard to believe today that hundreds of people were even burned at the stake because of their efforts to have the Bible translated. People like John Huss, William Tyndale and Archbishop Cranmer all paid this ultimate price so that people could have the Bible in their own languages.

It was not until 1604 that the most famous Bible translation of all time was authorized by King James of England. It was first published in 1611. With over a billion copies in print, it is the most printed book in the history of the world. And even though the language of the King James Bible is that of the early seventeenth century, it is still the preferred translation of many people today.

The Bible Today

Even though the Bible is available freely in most countries of the world, opposition to the Bible is not a thing of the ancient past. Even in our own lifetime huge prices have been paid by those who have smuggled Bibles to persecuted believers in nations where having a Bible is illegal. As a result, many have spent years in jail and many more have lost their lives.

The reason the Bible is opposed by the enemy of souls is because it contains words of life (see Psalm 119:50). How tragic it is that many people, even churchgoing Christians in countries where there is no shortage of Bibles, do not know what it contains and rarely, if ever, read it. Little do they realize what an enormous treasure they are ignoring.

Perhaps the biggest battle of all over the Bible is yet to be fought. That battle is getting all the people who are able to read it to actually do so.

Mahatma Gandhi, that great leader of the Indian people, was influenced strongly by Christianity in his younger days in South Africa. His brother became a Christian and went to the same church as my mother. But Gandhi could not stand hypocrisy in any form, and his tragic summation of the attitude of the Christians he had known toward the Bible is found in these words:

> You Christians look after a document containing enough dynamite to blow all civilisation to pieces, turn the world upside down and bring peace to a battle-torn planet. But you treat it is as though it is nothing more than a piece of literature.*

It is true that the Bible is great literature, but it is far more than that. It is the Bread of Life without which man cannot truly live. As we dig into the Bible together, we are going to unearth extraordinary and life-changing treasures. As the psalmist wrote in Psalm 119:105, "Your word is a lamp for my feet, a light on my path."

Living Bread

Today there are many English translations available, the most common of which is the New International Version. Alongside these are many others such as the New Revised Standard Version, the New King James Version, the New American Standard Bible, the Good News Translation and, more recently, the English Standard Version.

All these versions have their followings, and I have no intention of telling you which one to use. Most of the quotes in this book are from the New International Version.

*Mahatma Gandhi, "Mahatma Gandhi > Quotes > Quotable Quote," Goodreads, https://www.goodreads.com/quotes/456351-you-christians-look-after-a-document-containing-enough-dynamite-to.

In many ways it does not matter which version you read as long as you read it, take it in, digest it and live it. I find it helpful to read the Bible in several different versions. I have found it especially helpful to use a traditional translation as my main Bible and then to read one of the modern paraphrases such as the Good News Translation (Today's English Version) or The Living Bible to help me further understand what different passages are saying.

SUMMARY

The Bible is a miracle that was compiled over hundreds of years and inspired by the Holy Spirit of God. It has been opposed constantly by the enemy of souls because it is God's Word to a fallen world. It is the most precious thing anyone can possess and is God's timeless message to mankind.

PRAYER

Thank You, Lord, for those people who have given their lives so that the Bible could be made available for everyone to read. Help me to treasure this Book—the most precious and valuable thing that there has ever been and ever will be. I ask You to speak to me through it all of my days. In Jesus' name, Amen.

FEEDING ON THE LIVING BREAD

When I was young, I was encouraged to read a little bit of the Bible every day. It was a habit that became an important anchor point in my life. I honestly do not know where I would be today if it were not for the Word of God that has been hidden in my heart over many years.

I can remember times of temptation when a Scripture verse that I had learned years earlier would come suddenly into my mind. The psalmist understood this principle very well. In Psalm 119:11 he said, "I have hidden your word in my heart that I might not sin against you." What precious protection the Word of God is. It is living bread for the hungry soul.

I thank God that my parents cared enough to give me *Junior Notes*, the Scripture Union Bible reading notes for children. I learned to enjoy looking up the verse of the day, reading the little bit of teaching and saying the prayer. Sometimes it seemed as if there were too many things to do in the rush and tumble of school life, but I have never regretted the discipline and knowledge that was built into my life in this way, one step at a time and one day at a time.

Scripture in Song

I also learned Scripture through singing Christian songs at Sunday school and Bible class. Many had catchy tunes and words that were easy to remember. I absorbed a huge amount of Christian truth through them. They helped put the Bible into my heart.

Even today those songs come to memory easily, and they remind me of the simple truths that I have found to be thoroughly reliable over my seventy years. Simple truth that is believed firmly has a profound impact on the life of any man or woman. Few of those particular songs were great poetry or were set to great music, but they put the Word of God into my heart in an unforgettable way. To use the words of one of those choruses, I was feeding on the living bread.

In the eighteenth century, Charles Wesley put the preaching of his brother John into the lyrics of songs and came up with some of the most amazing hymns that have ever been written. He wrote hymns such as, "And Can It Be, That I Should Gain" and "Jesus, Lover of My Soul," both of which I am sure people will still be singing when Jesus comes again. They put the truths of Scripture into the hearts of people who learned the songs, sang the words and understood the truths described in the verses.

Hymns and songs have always been a great way of getting God's Word into the hearts of mankind. This method has been so successful that many songs of worship made their way into the Bible. The songs of King David (the psalms) are just that, and I have found that reading something from Psalms as part of my regular reading of the Word of God has always been a great blessing to me as well as a significant challenge.

The Need for Feeding

When we are young, we need food for two primary purposes. First, we need it for growth. Second, we need it for the energy we need to live each day. Malnourished children will never reach their physical potential. A regular supply of food in a well-balanced diet is essential both for growth and daily energy. When we are older, we still need food for daily living. We never grow out of the need for the right form of sustenance to keep us going.

God created us each with a spirit, soul and body. In exactly the same way as our bodies need feeding, so do our spirits and souls. Good parents talk to and play constantly with their children, teaching and training them as the years go by. They feed their souls. Little by little a baby becomes a toddler, a toddler becomes a child, a child becomes a young person and a young person becomes an adult. This happens not only in body but in knowledge, understanding, attitudes and responsibilities.

A child who is only fed physical food, but whose mind and emotions are not stimulated and who has not been trained in how to use their free will to make good choices, will grow up to be a very inadequate and deprived adult. This is obvious enough that even governments do everything they can to provide the necessary educational support services for parents. They do this so that when children grow up, they will be able to be a productive part of society.

What is necessary for the body and soul is also essential for the spirit. In fact, I would go as far as to say that if the spirit is not nurtured with the right sort of spiritual food, the effect will not only be on the spirit but on the soul and the body as well. A spirit that is nurtured in the things of God will protect the soul from making ungodly choices that can have devastating effects on every area of life.

There are all sorts of things that I could have gotten involved in as a young person, but I thank God that my early spiritual training meant that I had the courage to say no when attractive temptations presented themselves to me. It is only by the grace of God that I can now give testimony to His keeping power.

Not everyone is as fortunate. Every day, for example, we read of young people who are suffering because of drug overdoses, teenage pregnancies, binge drinking, sexually transmitted diseases or street violence. If their spirits had been nurtured, their consciences would have clicked into operation, and there would have been an inner strength from which they could draw to resist temptation.

In making decisions, they would have avoided the situations and relationships that led to, for example, partying where drugs were available.

Every day our newspapers are full of stories of what can happen to people when the Word of God has no influence in their lives.

We can have the most well-developed adult bodies and souls, but without the parallel development of our spirits we can never be powerful, mature and dynamic Kingdom people. We will always be vulnerable to the inroads of the enemy into our hearts and to the wrong choices that can often lead to disaster.

The psalmist expressed this powerfully when he said, "How can a young person stay on the path of purity? By living according to your word" (Psalm 119:9).

Taking in the Truth

The spirit needs food both for growth and for daily sustenance so that we will have the necessary spiritual energy to meet today's needs. This is not true simply when we are young or young in the faith but throughout our lives. Just as we cannot depend on yesterday's food for today's bodily energy, we cannot depend on yesterday's experiences of God to be sufficient for today's relationship with Him. We need to keep in touch with Him.

When people become Christians, at whatever age that might be, unless they are fed the right sort of spiritual food, they will remain as spiritual babes with a lot of growing to do. As such, they are very vulnerable and are in danger. Many former believers have fallen away from the faith because they did not have the opportunity to grow in their knowledge of God. In this life, we all have more to learn. We will never exhaust the knowledge of the things of God.

One of the fallacies exploited by the enemy is the assumption that if people become Christians when they are adults, they will not need as much training as those who become Christians as young children. The fact is that they need more. During their pre-Christian days, they have absorbed so much of the world's culture and standards that there can be a lot of relearning to do before real Christian growth becomes evident.

Paul's encouragement in Ephesians 4 for us to grow in maturity is an urgent call to the Body of Christ. He begins by warning us not to be tossed about on the uncertain waves of false doctrine or deception (see verse 14) and finishes with this declaration: "Instead, speaking the truth in love, we will grow to become in every respect the mature body of him who is the head, that is, Christ" (Ephesians 4:15).

The sad fact is that in today's churches we have a lot of believers who may be mature adults in every other way but who are babies when it comes to the things of the Spirit and the ways of God. I believe that the largest single reason that many have remained as spiritual babes and have not entered into their true destinies in God is because they have not learned to feed their spirits with a daily diet of the Word of God. Many have not been in churches where there is regular, systematic, Spirit-filled teaching from the Word of God to help people grow in the things of God.

In chapter 8 of Nehemiah we read of Ezra, the priest, bringing the people of God back to an understanding of the Law of God after a time of being away from Him. A special wooden platform (pulpit) was erected so that he could speak clearly to them and the people listened attentively. As the Law was spoken out, Ezra taught the people, "making it clear and giving the meaning so that the people understood what was being read" (verse 8). A good teacher will not only tell people what they are going to learn, but he will explain carefully its significance so that his listeners can really understand the importance of the teaching.

Let me give you an example. Most people know that one of the Ten Commandments instructs us not to commit adultery. What that does for many people is to make the idea of sexual temptation more attractive. Many of the people who attend Healing Retreats at Ellel Centers have had ungodly sexual relationships even though they knew what the Word of God said.

A number of years ago the Lord showed us how to teach what the consequences of sexual sin are and how people are still connected to previous sexual partners. I created a living example by inviting several people onto the stage. A man and a woman represented an engaged couple, and the others represented previous sexual partners of theirs.

I explained that for the purposes of this drama, we were to assume that both members of the couple had experienced premarital sex with multiple partners. I had some of the other people onstage hang onto the young couple as they prepared to get married, thus impeding their movement. The rest of the people held onto the limbs of the other sexual partners. This gave a visual for people to see how many different people can be tied onto a prospective marriage, and it showed how dangerous and long-lasting sexual sin is. The drama gave a great visual explanation as to why the Scriptures are clear about the need for sexual purity both before and after marriage.

Following this drama, a huge amount of personal repentance took place, including very significant healing in many lives. When people see the results of having permanent, ungodly soul ties that are established through sexual sin, they are quick to repent and seek God's forgiveness and healing. We will look at this more closely later in our journey to freedom.

I have lost count of the number of people who have said to me, "If only I had known these things when I was young—I would not now be living with the consequences of my mistakes."

In Nehemiah's day, the systematic teaching of the Law had an immediate effect. The people were joyful at what they heard but were also filled with conviction for their sin. This conviction led to repentance, forgiveness, worship and personal transformation. Lives were being changed, and people were growing up into maturity because they were now absorbing the Law of God (see Nehemiah 9:3). The Word of God was having an effect.

You will find it worthwhile to take some time to read chapters 8 and 9 of Nehemiah. It is a remarkable record of how people were transformed by the presence of God and by absorbing His Word.

Getting Started

I am praying that these lessons will be a tremendous help to you on your journey; however, they are not a substitute for reading the Word of God itself. Whenever a particular Scripture verse is mentioned, get your Bible out, look up the references and read them for yourself.

And may I make a plea to you? Never read the Bible without a pen, pencil or colored marker in your hand. Whenever you read something that has a particular impact on you, underline it or make a note in the margin. You will never regret being able to turn the pages of your Bible and be reminded of the things that God said to you in the past. The Bible will become your own personal tutorial book with God.

If you have a Bible that is a precious keepsake and you do not want to mark in it, get another one that you do not mind writing on. It is essential that you make note of what God says to you through His Living Word.

Some of my most precious possessions are my father's Bibles. They are covered with his own markings that detail God's working in his life. His markings are different than mine, and they are a precious reminder to me of my heritage. Making a record of important things God says to you is a key part of anyone's spiritual journey.

For many years I kept a personal spiritual diary where I recorded some of God's dealings with me. When I look back on those notes I can see the hand of God being traced through the ups and downs in my journey of life. Sometimes my diary was a letter to God in which I shared my heart with Him. At other times I would record things that I knew God had said to me, the questions I had for Him and various experiences of spiritual significance. There were also days when I wrote nothing, and that is all right, too.

You may like to go over what we have already shared together on our journey and make note of the things that have had an impact on you.

Next, we will look at ways of reading the Bible so that we can make sure that we take it all in. Every chapter matters to God and it must, therefore, matter to us. I trust that from this day on you will want to take in something of the Word of God every day.

SUMMARY

God wants us to grow into mature Christian believers. If we do not feed our spirit, however, we will remain spiritual babes and will not grow in our faith. Reading the Bible, which is written by the Holy Spirit, is the best way to learn about the ways of God and to be instructed on how to live a godly life.

PRAYER

Help me, Lord, never to forget that Your Word is a love letter to Your people. Help me to read it with the enthusiasm and excitement of knowing that You want to speak into my life and help me walk in Your ways. Help me also, Lord, never to forget the lessons I learned on this personal pilgrimage with You. In Jesus' name, Amen.

TAKING IT ALL IN

We have seen how important it is to feed daily on the living bread of the Word of God (see Deuteronomy 8:3; Matthew 4:4). The physical food you eat becomes part of your physical being, and what you feed on spiritually becomes part of your spiritual being. As you are intentional about eating good food and avoiding those things that would make you physically ill, you also need to take in good spiritual food and avoid the bad stuff that can have a negative impact on your life.

Many of the people who come to our centers for prayer are suffering the long-term consequences of bad spiritual food—everything from occult practices to the consequences of wrong choices. These things can become part of them, and they need help, healing and/or deliverance.

How do we take in the good and avoid the bad? In Philippians 4, Paul urged his readers to think about "whatever is true, whatever is noble, whatever is right, whatever is pure, whatever is lovely, whatever is admirable—if anything is excellent or praiseworthy—think about such things . . . and the God of peace will be with you" (verses 8 and 9).

This is wonderful advice and a wonderful promise. But how do we know the difference between the good and the bad? Sometimes they can look very much the same. We have to have a way of measuring the difference and sorting out the bad from the good.

We can look to the advice of experts. Experts are people who have a lot of experience and are able to give good advice based on their years of training and practical experience. Their field of expertise can be anything from financial affairs to tea tasting or gold refinement. Experts are paid a lot of money for their advice often simply because they have learned to know the difference between the good and the bad. They are advisers to those who need to benefit from what the experts know.

Our Resident Advisor

So how do we get such expert advice about spiritual things and the affairs of life? The key is having constant access to our own personal advisor, which is a wonderfully accurate name for the Holy Spirit.

Once we recognize that the ultimate author of the Bible is the Holy Spirit and that the Bible really is the Word of God, it makes a lot of sense to be diligent in reading it. And not just bits of it but all of it.

As we take it in, the Bible puts a straight edge of understanding into our spirits against which we can discern the difference between good and bad. The Holy Spirit becomes our resident advisor with the Bible as our reference book (see Hebrews 4:12).

Many times people have asked me for advice on all sorts of things having to do with living the Christian life. In perhaps ninety percent of these cases all I have had to do was give them advice they could have read for themselves in the Word of God. The problem for many was very simple. Because they were not reading God's Word, they did not know what was in it. They were not giving God the opportunity to give them His advice through reading His Word.

Max Reich, a Jew and a Messianic Believer in Yeshua (Jesus), summed it up this way: "The Christian who is careless in Bible reading will be careless in Christian living."* I can vouch a thousand times and more for the truth of this statement. Very often we have sought to help those who have been careless in Christian living because they were ignorant of what the Word of God actually said.

*Max Reich in Greg L. Bahnsen, *Pushing the Antithesis* (Powder Springs, Ga.: American Vision, 2007), 3.

D. L. Moody, who was a powerful American evangelist, once said, "Either the Bible will keep you away from sin, or sin will keep you away from the Bible!"*

The fact is that the more we take hold of the truth, the more that truth takes hold of us. It becomes part of our spiritual understanding. If our lives are in order with our spirits being led by the Holy Spirit and our souls and bodies taking their rightful place under the headship of the Spirit, then the understanding we have in our spirits will be like a permanent reference point of truth against which we can test all things (see 1 Thessalonians 5:21).

Andrew Murray, the extraordinary missionary saint who founded the South African General Mission and whose writings on prayer and many other topics from a hundred years ago are still bestsellers today, said, "Some read the Bible to learn and some read the Bible to hear from heaven."†

When we are able to hear from heaven through God's Word, we are able to use Scripture as a spiritual compass against which we can test the direction we are traveling. Without a compass, an explorer would get lost quickly. It is absolutely vital to know which direction you are traveling and then compare it to the direction you want to go. If there is a difference between what the compass says and the direction you are heading, you have problems. God gave us His Word so that we would have a permanent reference point to help us keep on course during life's journey.

Another way of looking at it is to consider that the Bible is the map and the Holy Spirit is the compass that shows you which way on the map to go. One without the other is relatively ineffective.

Promise-Box Christians

Promise boxes are not as common now as they used to be. My Aunty Gladys had one. In the box were hundreds of thin cards, and on every

---

*D. L. Moody, "Dwight L. Moody > Quotes > Quotable Quote," Goodreads, https://www.goodreads.com/quotes/668373-the-bible-will-keep-you-from-sin-or-sin-will.

†Andrew Murray, "Andrew Murray—Some read the Bible to learn . . .," The Ranch, posted March 8, 2008, http://theranch.org/2008/03/08/andrew-murray-some-read-the-bible-to-learn/.

one of them was a promise from the Bible. I used to enjoy picking one of the cards out of the box and seeing what Scripture passage I had selected. If I did not like it or did not understand it, I would put it back and try again.

Sadly, it is not only children who treat the Bible like that. If what people are reading confronts their behavior, they will often turn to something else instead of allowing the Holy Spirit to bring conviction and change (see James 1:22–25).

Each one of the promises in Aunty Gladys's box contained wonderful truths. With the benefit of hindsight, however, I can see that people should not depend on a promise box (or whatever its modern-day equivalent may be) for their daily intake of the Word of God. If they do, it is as though they are living off boxes of candied cherries and not eating any real food.

The promises of God are a bit like the cherries on a cake. They are wonderfully tasty, but if they are disconnected from the rest of the Word of God, they will create only an illusion. Even cherry cakes are not all cherry. The promises have relevance only when they are read within the context of when and how they were given, and they can be claimed only when we fulfill the conditions of the promise.

Popular and valuable equivalents of the promise box are devotional commentary books of daily readings. There are some very good ones. One of the best is one that my wife and I read from time to time. It is called *Morning and Evening* and is based on the writings of the great Victorian preacher Charles Spurgeon. We really enjoy reading it, and there have been occasions when the daily reading has been a particular blessing in our lives.

But Spurgeon would have been horrified if his book of daily readings had become a substitute for reading the Word of God. This is what he said about his own sermons from which the devotional volumes were compiled: "If my sermons kept people from reading the Bible for themselves, I would like to see the whole stock in a blaze and burned to ashes!"‡

---

‡Charles H. Spurgeon, "How to Become Full of Joy," *Spurgeon's Sermons*, vol. 51, *1911*, Christian Classics Ethereal Library, sermon originally published on October 19, 2011, posted on June 1, 2005, https://www.ccel.org/ccel/spurgeon/sermons57.xlii.html.

Spurgeon's *Morning and Evening* has 730 devotionals based on 730 verses from the Bible. There is one for the morning and one for the evening of each day of the year. But there are 1,189 chapters in the Bible and 31,273 verses. If you used Spurgeon's book every day (or any similar devotional volume) you would only ever read 2.33 percent of the Word of God. You would be hardly scratching the surface of the treasure that God has laid up for you in His Word.

While devotionals are excellent (Ellel Ministries has its own daily devotional called *Seeds of the Kingdom* available at www.seedsofthekingdom.com), they should never become a substitute for reading the Word of God.

I meet lots of Christians who can tell me some of their favorite Scripture verses, such as Psalm 23, John 3:16, Romans 8:28 or Revelation 3:20, but while these and other similar verses are precious and important, if that is all you know, there will be huge holes in your spiritual understanding. Promise-box Christians will know some of the truths of the Word of God, but their spirits will not contain the straight edge of God's Truth that comes from feeding regularly on living bread.

Here is some more insight from Spurgeon regarding Bible reading:

> The more you read the Bible and the more you meditate upon it, the more you will be astonished with it.*

> [The Bible] sanctifies and moulds the mind into the image of Christ.†

Reading It All

I hope by now you are understanding the message I am trying to get across. In essence it is that while there are wonderful texts in the Bible, many you may know by heart, you cannot live effectively as a disciple

---

*Charles H. Spurgeon, "Quotes on the Bible and on the Word," The Center for Biblical Studies, http://thecenterforbiblicalstudies.org/resources/quotes-on-the-bible-and-on-the-word/.

†Charles H. Spurgeon, *Spurgeon's Sermons*, vol. 17, *1871*, ed. Anthony Uyl (Woodstock, Ont.: Devoted Publishing, 2017), 375.

of Jesus with a promise-box mentality toward the Word of God. Unless you handle correctly the Word of truth (see 2 Timothy 2:15) and make the time to take in the whole of the Bible, you will miss out on much and you will not be "thoroughly equipped for every good work" (2 Timothy 3:17). It is the God-breathed Word of God that equips us for life.

Many years ago when I was taking my degree examinations, I studied every subject that I knew might come up in the exam paper. In reality, only about ten percent of the knowledge I had gained was necessary to pass the examination. But I had no idea which ten percent would be required of me. I could not take a chance and only learn ten percent of the material. That would have been a recipe for disaster. I had to learn it all so that I would be properly prepared for whatever I was asked. The result was that I passed the exam.

When it comes to the Bible, many Christians think that by knowing a few good texts they are equipped sufficiently for the trials and temptations of life. They are not. They need to take it all in so that whatever comes up in the "examination of life," they will be equipped fully for every situation and every good work that the Lord puts before them.

John Newton, the former slave ship captain who became an Anglican clergyman and wrote many wonderful hymns, including "Amazing Grace," turned to God in a terrible storm in which his ship nearly sank. He was close to meeting his maker. But God spared him, and during the rest of the voyage he began to read the Bible. It was an experience that marked the beginning of his pilgrimage to faith.

Many years later he said:

> I know not a better rule of reading the Scripture, than to read it through from beginning to end and when we have finished it once to begin again. We shall meet with many passages which we can make little improvement of, but not so many in the second reading as in the first, and fewer in the third than in the second: provided we pray to him who has the keys to open our understandings, and to anoint our eyes with His spiritual ointment.‡

‡John Newton, "Quotes on the Bible and on the Word," The Center for Biblical Studies, http://thecenterforbiblicalstudies.org/resources/quotes-on-the-bible-and-on-the-word/.

There are two principles that John Newton is drawing our attention to. The first one is that we should read all of the Bible whether we understand it or not. The second one is that we should always pray that the Holy Spirit will give us understanding of what is written. One of the earliest prayers I can remember learning is one my dad taught me to pray as a child. It is found in Psalm 119:18. "Open my eyes that I may see wonderful things in your law."

Among the peoples of the world, Christians have a unique privilege. They are able to read their favorite book and simultaneously talk to the author and ask Him to explain its meaning.

How Do I Read It All?

If some of you are thinking that reading right through the Bible is too hard for you, let me tell you about Hannah. She first came to Ellel Grange in her early twenties. She had experienced years of abuse that damaged her spirit terribly.

God brought her a lot of healing, but when she returned home she had to manage her life with God's help. She found that reading the Bible every day was the best thing she could do. She did not always understand what she was reading, but day by day she felt herself getting stronger. She made the Word of God her own. This is what she said:

> Because of what happened to me, the doctors said I was a psychotic depressive. But Jesus said, "I am the way, the truth and the life." He is also the Alpha and Omega, the first and the last. I knew He had something better for me.
>
> One morning I decided that I was going to read the whole Bible in a year. It was not very easy to read it every day, but it was the best thing I ever did! As I read the Bible, I learned a lot—and I struggled a lot, but I knew Jesus was always there for me. It says, "Knock and the door will be opened." It was for me! So, go on, knock and see how close Jesus comes to you. I hope your experience is as good as mine. Jesus never lets us down.

SUMMARY

It is clear from Scripture that Jesus accepted the Old Testament as being the inspired Word of God. And the same is true for the New Testament—it is God-breathed. Making a plan to read the whole Bible one step at a time is a vital part of our Christian pilgrimage.

PRAYER

Lord, I want to learn from Your Word day by day. Forgive me for times when I have chosen not to read the Bible and have missed out on much of what You wanted me to understand. Help me, Lord, to read the most precious book in the world as Your gift to me and the whole of mankind. In Jesus' name, Amen.

GUIDANCE FOR DAILY LIVING

I have more people ask me about guidance than probably almost any other topic. It is great that many people are eager to know what God's will is for their lives. It is, however, also alarming that such a high proportion of these people have been Christians for a long time and yet have never learned how to listen to God's voice for themselves.

Many want to know about guidance, but they do not want to persevere and do the work of developing a relationship with the guide. If we do not know the guide, how can we receive His guidance?

It seems that many people have decided that they would prefer to get a word for their lives from someone else rather than hear the voice of God for themselves. This is really dangerous. If we do not know how to let God speak to us directly through His Word, how can we ever test what other people might be saying to us?

Sadly, there are many people today who are waiting for God to fulfill a word that might not have been from Him in the first place. No wonder Scripture commands us to test all things (see 1 Thessalonians 5:21). Testing is not necessary when something is obviously ungodly and bad. We can reject those things. Testing is for the things that look, sound and even feel good.

Satan will not try initially to deceive us through things that are obviously bad and wrong. He is far too subtle for that. He will try to deceive us and lead us astray through things that seem acceptable and good. Satan's good is always the enemy of God's best. Scripture warns us that Satan sometimes masquerades as an angel of light (see 2 Corinthians 11:14).

Guidance for Life

There are dozens of verses that talk about the way God speaks to us and that show us the way to go. One of my favorites is Isaiah 30:21: "Whether you turn to the right or to the left, your ears will hear a voice behind you, saying, 'This is the way; walk in it.'"

Perhaps the most well-known guidance Scripture is Proverbs 3:6: "In all your ways submit to him, and he will make your paths straight." When Jesus was teaching the disciples about the work of the Holy Spirit in John 16:13, He said, "When he, the Spirit of truth, comes, he will guide you into all the truth."

In each of these well-known verses, the emphasis is on God speaking directly to us about the conduct of our lives leading us into what is true and right. While there may be times when God speaks clearly through others (and there have been some important occasions like this in my own life), we must learn to know and follow the voice of God for ourselves. We should not depend solely on what others might say. There are times when we are on our own and out of contact with Christian friends. Unless we have learned to recognize and follow the voice of the Lord, we could be in deep trouble.

Avoiding Deception

In these very testing days, it is absolutely essential for us to be able to differentiate between what is true and what is false. We need to be able to recognize deception for what it is. Learning to know the voice of God in the midst of many competing voices and obeying that voice are important foundational keys to living the Christian life.

There is a story of eastern shepherds from various regions who brought their sheep to a watering hole and sat and talked while their flocks drank. After the flocks had drunk their fill, the shepherds prepared to go on their separate ways to find fresh grazing for their sheep. How would they manage to separate out their flocks again? They were mingled together to the point that it was impossible to identify which sheep belonged to which flock.

When the shepherds got up and left the watering hole traveling in four different directions, they spoke to their sheep. As if by some magical prearranged signal, the flocks separated themselves and each one followed their own shepherd. No human sorting was necessary.

The event was not as miraculous as it looked. It was simply that the sheep had grown accustomed to listening to the voice of their own shepherd. All the shepherd had to do was talk to his sheep. Guidance for the sheep was simply a matter of recognizing their own shepherd's voice and following him.

In a very similar way, it is vital that we learn to recognize the voice of our own Shepherd (see John 10:27) and understand His ways. The more we read the Word of God, the more we will understand the ways of God. Knowing that God will not lead us on a path that is contrary to His ways gives us confidence to be able to trust Him, especially when we sense Him leading us in a particular direction.

If we do not know what is in the Word of God, then we will not have any means of testing what we think God is saying to us. This is what God said to Joshua when he was taking on responsibility for leading God's people following the death of Moses: "Keep this Book of the Law always on your lips; meditate on it day and night, so that you may be careful to do everything written in it. Then you will be prosperous and successful" (Joshua 1:8).

Meditating on the Word

God's instruction to Joshua was to meditate on God's laws. Meditation is a spiritual equivalent of carefully chewing a favorite food. We take our time to enjoy it and savor it.

In the same way, God asks us to carefully digest His Word so that we can understand what it means and can learn how to apply it in our lives. This is what I do when I am trying to understand something fresh from God's Word.

First, I pray a simple prayer based on the words from Psalm 119:18: *Open my eyes that I can really see and understand what you are saying to me through this passage from your Word.*

Then I read the passage two or sometimes three times. Each time I try to read it from a different perspective.

When you compare a picture of a building taken from one angle to a picture of the same building taken from a different angle you may be surprised at how different it looks. When the perspective changes, the picture changes. In a similar way, I first look at a passage and ask myself how it seems from my own perspective. Then I read it again and put myself in God's shoes and try to see it afresh from His perspective. I then read around the passage to see what came before and what came after, and I look up any cross-references to other verses that my Bible provides.

Finally, if what I am reading is about people and there are different characters in the passage, I might read the story again, putting myself in their shoes, trying to see things from their perspective. When you read the stories of Jesus' encounters with either Nicodemus or Zacchaeus, for example, and you see them from their different perspectives, you get a whole new insight into what was happening.

I look to see what is relevant to me first, and then after having taken in everything, I can pray about any particular things that I sensed God was saying to me.

Sometimes God is saying something to me for that day through the passage I am reading. Most times, however, I am storing up understanding in my personal library of faith so that at some future time of need I can draw on the treasure that I have now made my own.

Testing a Word from the Lord

The entire Bible contains the Word of God because it is the Word of God, but there are times when a specific Scripture will jump off of the page in such a powerfully relevant way that we recognize it is as being more than part of the biblical record. At that moment, something from the written Word becomes a specific word from God into our lives for now.

Such a word can come to us in many different ways. In my own experience, it has sometimes been spoken out by a preacher who is quoting a Scripture passage in a sermon. At other times, Scripture has had an impact on my spirit suddenly as I read the Bible for myself. And then again a verse I may have learned many years ago comes into my memory for no other reason than God was using it to speak to me in my present situation.

The first time God spoke to me about what He wanted me to do with my life was when I started to restore a broken car and found that the chassis was bent. As I looked at the chassis, I sensed God saying to me that I could restore the car, but that He could restore broken lives.

Then He asked me the question, *Which is more important?*

Obviously broken lives are more important than broken cars. The Bible talks about God restoring broken lives. What I sensed God was saying to me was consistent with what I already knew was in Scripture— and that is the first stage in testing a word from God. Is it consistent with the general message of Scripture?

Jesus' personal mission statement was taken from Isaiah 61:1. He quoted this passage to the congregation in His own synagogue in Nazareth. He said that He had come to heal the brokenhearted and to set the captives free. Then in Luke 9:1–2, Jesus sent out His disciples to preach the Kingdom, heal the sick and cast out demons.

The word I sensed that God had spoken to me was, therefore, not only consistent with the life and ministry of Jesus but also with what Jesus had asked His disciples to do. A number of years later when I sensed that the time was coming when God was about to open up the ministry that I had seen in a vision, Ruth Hawkey, who was a visiting preacher at my local Methodist church, spoke about Abraham going out in faith but not knowing where he was going. As she preached, the vision that God had given me for a healing ministry was burning within me.

It was as if a dormant seed was bursting suddenly into life at that moment. I knew God was telling me to start moving forward in faith even though I did not know where that would lead. Through what Ruth was saying, God spoke directly into my spirit.

On the way out of the church, I spoke to Ruth about what God had said to me through her sermon. She shared with me the other side of the story. She knew that God had given her that specific word for someone at that service, but she did not know for whom. She then gave me the other part of the word she had received. She quoted John 2:5 that says, "Do whatever he tells you."

As Ruth spoke out those words, it was as if a starting pistol went off in my head. The time had come. The vision that I had been nurturing and believing in for years really must have been from God, and the time for its fulfillment was coming soon. God was giving me clear direction through His Word to go and do what Jesus had spoken into my heart.

The preacher that day was simply being obedient to what God had given her, and her obedience was a very significant moment in my own pilgrimage. I still know Ruth, over thirty-five years after that event, and she remembers it well. She and her husband, Joe, have been much-loved visiting teachers in our schools.

Filling in the Details—Luke 9:11

God can not only use Scripture to point us in the general direction we should go but to also help us with some of the details. Let me illustrate from my own experience how God used specific Scripture passages to speak into my life.

As the vision for the work of Ellel Ministries grew, I began to seek the Lord more specifically. What, for example, would this work actually look like? At that time I knew very little about the healing ministry, but the desire to see people healed by God burned deeply in my heart.

I began to read Scripture with a greater sense of purpose, looking for God's answers to my questions. My Bible was marked liberally with everything that God was teaching me about healing. As I read the Word of God, the vision for Healing Retreats was born in my spirit.

I believed that people would not only come for prayer but would also receive teaching to help put a solid foundation into their lives. But what would I teach about on these retreats?

I started looking specifically for all the teaching Jesus gave about how to get healed. To my shock and amazement I could not find any. I now had a problem in that I had no real concrete direction on how to run a healing retreat.

I searched Scripture again and systematically scoured the gospels for clues. As I read Luke 9, I came to the story of the feeding of the five thousand. Some words I had never noticed before had a deep impact on me. All of my previous focus in this passage had been on what Jesus did to feed the five thousand, but not on what He was doing with them before He fed them.

God was opening my eyes. Luke 9:11 tells what He had been doing previously: "He welcomed them and spoke to them about the kingdom of God, and healed those who needed healing."

As I read these words, it seemed as though they were standing out from the page. God had my attention. I meditated on this simple statement, and as I did, it was as if I was hearing the voice of the Lord speaking clearly into my heart about how He wanted the ministry to be run.

First, people needed to be welcomed warmly, because a sincere welcome communicates love to the stranger. When people feel loved, they are much more likely to listen to what is being taught. When I thought about it, it seemed obvious. It is a simple concept, yet it is also very profound.

Then after the people had been welcomed and loved, they needed to be taught. The teaching we needed to give them was not teaching about how to get healed but about the Kingdom of God. The Lord was showing me something very significant: If the foundational principles of living a godly life under the Lordship of Jesus are not in a person's life, then it will be very hard for people either to receive or to keep the healing they need.

And finally, we needed to pray for healing. After a person knows they are welcomed and loved and after they have some understanding of key principles of Kingdom living, they should be ready to be healed.

The foundational principles for the ministry, which was established in 1986, were designed through a specific word from God from Luke

9:11. As the Ellel teams have ministered around the world on literally thousands of three-day Healing Retreats, we have seen God do extraordinary things in people's lives. We have seen people make huge strides forward in their Christian pilgrimages.

The Living Word

The writer of the book of Hebrews summed up how the Word of God can operate in our lives: "For the word of God is alive and active. Sharper than any double-edged sword, it penetrates even to dividing of soul and spirit, joints and marrow; it judges the thoughts and attitudes of the heart" (4:12).

In our journey we will be referring constantly to Scripture. We will experience firsthand how God uses His Word to speak directly into our lives and how He leads us into the plans and purposes He has laid out for us.

SUMMARY

God's Word is the most powerful means through which He guides and directs His people. Once you get the Word in your heart, the Holy Spirit can use it. As the days of your life move forward, you can listen to what God is saying through His Word and apply it in your life. But as you wait on Him, you also have to persevere in your relationship and exercise faith. You can then watch God work miracles of His grace within and through you.

PRAYER

Help me, Lord, to have my eyes opened to see the wonderful truths that are in the Word of God. Help me to have spiritual ears that are alert to hear what it is that You are saying to me as I read Your Word, day by day. In Jesus' name, Amen.

ENCOURAGEMENT AND **INSPIRATION** AT ALL TIMES

I am trusting that by now you have understood something of my heart for you. My deepest concern is that you would not miss out on developing a personal and life-transforming relationship with the living God. It is a relationship in which you can trust Him completely every step of the way, whatever the circumstances of life and whatever He asks you to do for Him.

I have been writing this guidebook during a very difficult season in my own life. It is a season in which I have had to put what I have been teaching to the test. I had to say an earthly good-bye to someone with whom I have walked for many years as a brother in the ministry. While my friend Norman may no longer be with us in an earthly sense, he is still very much with us in a spiritual sense. He is now joined to Christ in eternity, and we are joined to Christ in time. Jesus is the bridge between one side of the curtain of death and the other, between time and eternity.

None of us knew that his home-call would be as sudden as it was, but in all the circumstances surrounding his passing, it has been abundantly clear to everyone that God was in charge.

Shortly before he died, he wrote,

> I have experienced for myself, deep in my spirit, the reality of Jesus' love and peacefulness. My life is safe and secure—I have known it all my life in my thoughts—but now I know it like a solid foundational rock, securely placed in my spirit. A rock of experience—not just knowledge, strong enough to build my life on.

How can someone feel safe and secure in Jesus at a time of such personal crisis? The answer in his case was that over a long period of time, he had developed a close relationship with God and had fed on His Word. He made it his own. His writings were impregnated with the truths of Scripture, and for many, many years they had been a constant source of encouragement and inspiration to him. He had taken in spiritual food, and the food had become part of him.

His life was founded on the Rock of Jesus Christ. My aim is that through JOURNEY TO FREEDOM you will become established more firmly on that solid and totally dependable Rock.

Encouragement

The word *encouragement* is a friendly word. We like it because it gives us a sense of security and well-being. When we are encouraged, we feel better immediately and are strengthened in whatever we are doing. And when things are difficult, a person who encourages us is always a welcome friend. A person with the opposite message can soon depress and undermine us until we become vulnerable to the temptation of giving up.

But what does the word *encouragement* really mean? While we understand what a blessing words of encouragement are, sometimes the real meaning of words gets lost in changing circumstances or understanding. If you have come to associate the word *encouragement* with a pat on the back to comfort you and make you feel better, you have not understood its real meaning. You have missed the point of how the word is used in Scripture.

The real meaning of *encouragement* is associated with the words *courage* and *bravery*. It is not associated with a comforting pat on the back. The word *bravery* implies a successful completion of a task in the face of danger, even great danger. A brave person is someone who does not turn back when things get tough.

Encouragement is associated more with giving strength for battle than making someone feel better with a few kind words. Initially, words of real encouragement (giving courage to) may not make you feel any better, but they will give you the strength to push through to do something you may even be frightened of.

One of the greatest encouragers of all time was Winston Churchill. He was voted "the man of the century" by the British people. He was the prime minister during World War II, and largely through his remarkable leadership, the British people were able to lead the Allied Forces to a great victory in that awful conflict.

When he was appointed prime minister, he did not try to soften the situation with comforting words. He did not give either Parliament or the people a gentle pat on the back to give them false encouragement. He set before them the reality of what the nation was facing. He did not cover up the horrors of war, but rather spoke about the situation as it was. One might have thought that such blunt talk would have had a negative effect, but in reality it did the very opposite. People were given courage to fight.

Here is some of what Churchill said in two of his most famous speeches:

> I have nothing to offer but blood, toil, tears and sweat. We have before us an ordeal of the most grievous kind. We have before us many, many long months of struggle and of suffering. You ask, what is our policy? I can say: It is to wage war, by sea, land and air, with all our might and with all the strength that God can give us; to wage war against a monstrous tyranny, never surpassed in the dark, lamentable catalogue of human crime. That is our policy. You ask, what is our aim? I can answer in one word: It is victory, victory at all costs, victory in spite of all terror, victory, however long and hard the road may be; for without victory, there is no survival.*

---

*Winston Churchill, "Blood, Toil, Tears and Sweat," International Churchill Society, May 13, 1940, https://winstonchurchill.org/resources/speeches/1940-the-finest-hour/blood-toil-tears-and-sweat-2/.

We shall go on to the end, we shall fight in France, we shall fight on the seas and oceans, we shall fight with growing confidence and growing strength in the air, we shall defend our Island, whatever the cost may be, we shall fight on the beaches, we shall fight on the landing grounds, we shall fight in the fields and in the streets, we shall fight in the hills; we shall never surrender.†

These speeches set the tone for the years of conflict ahead, and they prepared people for battle. They gave people courage because they now knew there was a man in charge of the nation who knew what he was doing. It gave them confidence that even though the fight may be long and hard, it was a battle worth fighting. In short, the people were given courage—they were encouraged.

It was about three thousand years earlier that a relatively young man was commissioned to take up the reins of leadership from Moses. Moses was not going to be able to enter the Promised Land himself, so this assignment was given to Joshua.

Moses was instructed to "commission Joshua, and encourage and strengthen him, for he will lead this people across and will cause them to inherit the land that you will see" (Deuteronomy 3:28). This assignment from the living God to take His people across the River Jordan to occupy the land was not an easy one. To achieve this huge objective, battles would have to be fought. Some battles would be against fearsome peoples in a land where giants lived (see Numbers 13:32).

God knew that Joshua would need all the courage he could muster. After Moses died, God said to Joshua, "Be strong and courageous" (Joshua 1:6). He reinforced this message in verse 7 by adding the word *very*. He told Joshua to "Be strong and very courageous." In the boldest words of encouragement, He told Joshua, "Be strong and courageous. Do not be afraid; do not be discouraged, for the LORD your God will be with you wherever you go" (verse 9).

---

†Winston Churchill, "We Shall Fight on the Beaches," International Churchill Society, June 4, 1940, https://winstonchurchill.org/resources/speeches/1940-the-finest-hour/we-shall-fight-on-the-beaches/.

This was God's way of encouraging Joshua. He told him the reality of the situation, but at the same time assured Joshua of His presence wherever he went. It is the presence of God that we all need desperately to have. What a massive difference it makes to know that God is with us. That is the ultimate seal of encouragement for every situation in life we might have to face.

When David discovered that the Amalekites had carried off all of the women from his village and that his own men were turning against him, what did he do? First Samuel 30:6 tells us that "David found strength in the LORD his God."

He went to the God who had promised to be with him and drew courage from on high. David's relationship with God was such that he knew exactly what to do. He went to Him for encouragement. He took courage and was able to press on. In a remarkable victory that followed, he recovered everyone and everything that had been taken.

Encouragement can be defined as being strengthened by God for the battles of life. In Ephesians 6, Paul described the Christian life using warfare as an example, and in the dramatic word picture that he painted we are under constant threat from the enemy of souls. In other places, he referred to the Christian life as an endurance race.

Whatever picture fits best, you must realize that without courage you will neither be able to fight spiritual battles or endure in the marathon race of life. Scripture is your best possible source of courage. It is the vitamin pill, the spiritual glucose and the solid food that will equip you for the journey ahead.

In Churchill's speeches of encouragement during World War II he left no room whatsoever for the possibility of defeat. He knew that no matter how long the battle would rage, victory would come. In the same way we can be encouraged to know that because Jesus overcame Satan at the cross, we, too, can be certain of victory over all the powers of darkness. The Word of God encourages us to be steadfast and immoveable and by faith hold the ground. Jesus is our Rock, the sure foundation in which we can put our trust (see Hebrews 6:18–19).

Inspiration

When you breathe you inspire—meaning that you expand your lungs and take in breath. Spiritually, when you are inspired, you take on board the breath of God and allow Him to be the source of hope and strength for the challenges of life.

I like this definition of *inspire*: "to infuse with an encouraging or exalting divine influence, to bring about a change in the heart and will of one's hearers; to energize the soul with the influence of God."

I just love those last few words—"energize the soul with the influence of God." That is exactly what the Holy Spirit does for us. He equips us with strength and courage, and He energizes our souls.

It is hard to separate out the two important words of *encouragement* and *inspiration*. They are two sides of the same coin. When we are inspired by the Holy Spirit, we are energized by God. And when we are encouraged by God, it is always to do those things that He has inspired us to do.

Problems arise in our Christian walks when we try to live from our own strength. Oftentimes we do things that God has not asked us to do and for which God cannot give us the courage. This is what happens when people believe falsely that something has been inspired by God when it has not. People use all of their energy and resources trying to be obedient to a false vision. Often they finish up very disillusioned and discouraged. Sometimes they even get angry with God and blame Him for not doing what they wanted Him to do.

This is why it is important to test even those things that seem to come from God. You must learn how to recognize and avoid the deceptions of the enemy.

When Jesus faced Satan during His wilderness experience, He countered the temptation to turn stones into bread by saying, "Man shall not live on bread alone, but on every word that comes from the mouth of God" (Matthew 4:4). In John 6:63, Jesus said, "The Spirit gives life; the flesh counts for nothing. The words I have spoken to you—they are full of the Spirit and life." In these Scripture passages Jesus was underlining how critical it is that we live by inspiration. As we breathe in the Word of God from the heart of God, it gives us life. What a privilege, what a blessing!

Comfort

I do not want to leave our look at the Bible without mentioning the word *comfort*. While encouragement is giving courage, comfort is showing care, compassion and understanding. These are all an outworking of the fact that God is love. They are expressions of the heart of God toward His children.

In the Bible we read about the God of all comfort (see 2 Corinthians 1:3). We read of the compassion of God when He says, "Blessed are those who mourn, for they will be comforted" (Matthew 5:4), and of His wishes for the people who love Him, "Comfort, comfort my people" (Isaiah 40:1).

God really does want us to know the precious comfort of His loving presence in the deepest recesses of our souls. One of the very best ways to know that comfort is to make meditation on the Word of God a lifelong habit. As you think about the things God has said to us in His precious Word, His comfort becomes as natural as breathing.

I have known some very difficult times in my own life, and I have been amazed at how God draws living water for me out of the deep well of His Word. This living water has comforted me in my innermost being. God has come to me at my most vulnerable and hurting times and wrapped me in spiritual cotton as He brought healing balm to my soul. Throughout Scripture the comfort of God is evident, and the psalms are especially full of His comforting words.

Every day as you read God's Word more gems are added to your spiritual understanding. You do not have to worry about remembering them all. If you get them in, the Holy Spirit will get them out exactly when you need them.

At All Times

Scripture is a constant source of encouragement, inspiration and comfort. When we are facing challenges and temptation, the Word from God comes to us. And as the psalmist reminds us, the God of Israel does not fall asleep (see Psalm 121:4). He is always ready and willing to hear our cry and answer our prayer.

To be in a relationship means we also need to know how to communicate. In the next part of our journey, we will go to the very center of how we relate to God. We will look at how we can both speak to Him and hear His voice. Prayer is not just something we do when we decide to pray. It needs to become a 24/7 experience.

I pray that as you think over all of the topics that we have shared about the Bible, you will be able to look at God's Word in a very different way.

As I said at the beginning of this stage, "Without a map, I get lost. Without the Bible, I am lost before I even begin the journey."

With the Bible, you have the map in your hand, and with the Holy Spirit in your heart, you have the key to understanding it. Take it all in, store it up and then live it out for the rest of your days. The Bible is truly the most precious thing that exists on the planet. It contains the keys to life.

SUMMARY

The Bible is a constant source of courage for life's journey. Through its pages, God encourages us and inspires us to live for Him. Without the Bible, we are lost, we have no true knowledge of the living God and we are ill-equipped to do the works of the Kingdom of God.

PRAYER

Lord, I do not want to have the false comfort of being patted on the back when what I really need is Your courage to live the Christian life. I pray that starting today You will give me fresh inspiration from Your heart to mine and encourage me in all that I seek to do for You. In Jesus' name, Amen.

STAGE 4

THE VITAL BREATH OF PRAYER

Prayer is the blood that flows in the artery that connects God's heart to mine.

PRAYER—THE CHRISTIAN'S VITAL BREATH

If you own a car, it is absolutely essential that you know how to fill it up with fuel. Cars without fuel are useless museum pieces that are going nowhere. And Christians who do not know how to pray are like cars without fuel. They are in danger of becoming museum pieces that are occupying space in the church, out of touch with God and going nowhere.

Many hymn writers have tried to express the nature of prayer in their poetry. In my opinion none has done so more effectively than James Montgomery. He was a Scottish contemporary of John Wesley. His parents were Moravian missionaries in the West Indies who died when James was very young.

He was a brave man who went through many difficult times, including two stints in prison for having had the courage to publish articles and poems in support of the great causes of his day, including the abolition of slavery. He needed to know how to pray. Some of the greatest hymns are from his pen.

The Air We Breathe

It was James Montgomery who coined the phrase "the Christian's vital breath." In his hymn "Prayer Is the Soul's Sincere Desire," he includes these remarkable words: "Prayer is the Christian's vital breath, the Christian's native air."*

In describing prayer as "vital breath" and "the Christian's native air," he expressed a profound truth about prayer. Praying should be as natural and as essential as breathing. If we cease to breathe, we begin to die, and if we cease to pray, our relationships with God can begin to die.

The apostle Paul expressed a similar thought when he wrote in 1 Thessalonians 5:17 that we should "pray continually." In the King James Version of the Bible, Paul's words are translated "pray without ceasing." Words like these invite a challenge. How can we possibly be constantly in prayer and also fulfill the normal routines of life? Surely we must also concentrate on the business of living, working, being with family and having leisure time. How it is possible that we can pray at all times?

What if I were to say to you, "How can I constantly breathe and also fulfill the normal routines of life? I cannot possibly do all of these other things and breathe at the same time." I am sure you would simply laugh at my stupidity. Everyone knows that if you do not breathe you cannot live, move or do anything.

Breathing is of greater importance than all of the other physical things in the world that you might like to do. Without breath you will have no oxygen, and without oxygen your body cannot function and you will die. Breathing has to be of higher priority than every other function of life. We do not have to think about it. We breathe as we go about our daily routines. It is an automatic process.

This is the message that James Montgomery and the apostle Paul were both trying to get across in regard to prayer. Prayer is the oxygen of the spirit and the soul. It is the channel of access to the heart of God and the channel of blessing from the throne of God. It is of greater importance than anything else we do. If we do not pray, we are cutting ourselves off from the supply line of grace. This leaves us as helpless as a fish out of water that is flopping on the river bank, waiting to die.

*James Montgomery, "Prayer Is the Soul's Sincere Desire," Hymnal.net, https://www.hymnal.net/en/hymn/h/761.

A 24/7 Prayer Meeting

Clearly, if prayer is to be considered as important as breathing, we have to dispense with the idea that we can pray only at certain times or in certain places, such as prayer meetings, at the beginning or end of the day or when we say "amen" to what the minister says in church on a Sunday morning.

I am not saying that corporate prayer at prayer meetings is not important—it is. Nor am I saying that the prayers at church services do not matter—they do. But what I am saying is that if we have not learned how to live and breathe the air of prayer, then much of our other praying will be as lifeless as a set of lungs without oxygen.

If it is true that we can never escape from the presence of God (see Psalm 139:7–12), then it is also true that God is always there to fellowship with us in prayer. He cannot escape from our presence, either.

Brother Lawrence, the seventeenth-century French monk whose writings were compiled into one of the most well-known Christian books on prayer called *The Practice of the Presence of God*, put it this way: "You need not cry very loud; He is nearer to us than we are aware of."†

A relationship with God is like a 24/7 prayer meeting forever. He is always there, and He is never absent from the meeting. He loves to enjoy your company, and He loves for you to enjoy His company.

The key foundation stone of a life of prayer is constant awareness of the presence of God. He is interested in what we are doing and wants us to participate in what He is doing.

There are many great men and women of God with whom I would have loved to meet and from whom I would have loved to learn. High on my list of such people would have been that great Indian saint of God, Sadhu Sundar Singh.

He said that prayer "is the desire for God Himself" and that "the true spirit of prayer does not consist in asking God for blessings, but in receiving Him who is the giver of all blessings, and in living a life of fellowship with Him."‡ He was absolutely right.

---

†Brother Lawrence, *The Practice of the Presence of God* (New York: Start Publishing, 2012), 35.

‡Sadhu Sundar Singh, "Sadhu Sundar Singh," Great Thoughts Treasury, www.greatthoughtstreasury.com/author/sadhu-sundar-singh.

As you read the Bible, you realize that constant fellowship with the Father was the most important thing in Jesus' life. He did only what the Father told Him to do (see John 5:19). He went only where the Father told Him to go. He said only what the Father told Him to say. How did He know how to do these things? Because He lived in that precious 24/7 relationship with God that is the essence of prayer.

In any close relationship, you do not have to talk constantly to remain in the relationship. You are in relationship whether or not you are speaking. Either of you can open up a conversation at any time. You do not have to request permission to speak or go to a special place for a meeting before you can start a conversation. You can start a conversation at anytime, anywhere.

In Ephesians, Paul uses the marriage relationship to paint a picture of the relationship between Jesus and the people who form the Church (see Ephesians 5:22–33). Jesus is described as the Bridegroom and the Church as His bride. It is clearly God's intention that the relationship between His people and Himself was meant to be an intimate one in which both parties participate constantly.

A relationship with God is also a bit like a telephone call that goes on forever. Neither of you puts the receiver down. The line is held open for time and eternity, and the calls are free.

It is through prayer that we keep in touch with our heavenly Father. It is through prayer that He shares with us His vision for our lives. It is through prayer that we bring our needs and circumstances to Him. It is through prayer that we can express our love to Him. It is through prayer that we can hear His gentle voice bringing encouragement, correction or direction. It is through prayer that we talk to Him about things we do not understand, such as passages in the Bible or the circumstances and events of our lives.

I could go on and on about all of the things that are achieved through prayer—that intimate, spiritual fellowship between God and His children. But now we are going to look at some important aspects of prayer that were highlighted by Jesus in what we call the Lord's Prayer.

Getting a Right Perception of God as a Loving Father

Before we can proceed further with our study of prayer, it is vital that you understand something very significant about the nature and character of God. Unless you have a right understanding of what He is like, you will not feel comfortable about the sort of intimate relationship with God that I am encouraging you to have.

I once said to a lady who had experienced a very difficult upbringing that she needed to really know the loving care of God, her heavenly Father.

The moment I said this she turned on me sharply and literally spat the words out of her lips, "Do not ever talk to me about God being a father. If He is anything like my father, I just do not want to know Him."

It took me a while to understand why her reaction had been violent, but when she told me her story, I began to understand. Her father had been abusive and would beat her and her brothers and sisters regularly for no reason. He would go out drinking most nights, and when he came home drunk he would beat all of the children.

To escape this tyranny, one of them would sit up and wait until he or she could see their dad coming down the road outside. The child on guard would then wake the others, and they would all rush out into the backyard and lock themselves in a coal shed, hiding there until their dad fell asleep.

"That is what fathers are like," the woman said.

She had a major problem. She assumed that what her father had been like was representative of what all fathers are like—even God the Father. She had grown up with this belief in her heart, and there was no way she was ever going to respond to any prayer that addressed God as Father.

My own childhood experience was the very opposite of this. As a result, I grew up knowing that talking to God as Father was safe. I learned about prayer from a mom and dad who prayed and included their children in their process of prayer.

But many, many people have a major problem with prayer. In most cases, this is not because they disagree with the idea of prayer, but rather because their image of what God is like has been distorted by their own human father. It is impossible for them to relate to God as a Father in a loving way.

As we have already seen, it was God's intention that human parenting would be the way that one generation after another received a true picture of the nature and the character of God. In this way, all generations would understand how much the Father God loves His children. They would have learned about what good fathers are like from their own parents.

But man fell into sin. Satan became the god of this world and became known as the father of lies.

In John 8:42–47, Jesus addressed some of the wicked religious leaders of His day. He said that they were behaving as their father the devil and were carrying out his desires. When people do bad things, it is important to realize that they are not doing these things because they are behaving like their heavenly Father, but that they are behaving like Satan, who is a false god and a false father.

God designed children to learn about Him from their parents, therefore, children believe instinctively that the way they were treated is the way God would treat them. When we meet people who do not believe God is interested in them, it is often because they had a father who was interested only in himself.

Some believe that God must be far too busy to be interested in them because that is exactly how their human fathers behaved. This can even be the case with Christian fathers who are too busy with the things of God to spend time with the gifts of God (their children).

Others look to God as a sort of Father Christmas who is there to give them presents from an eternal Christmas tree. This is because their own human fathers gave presents to them, often as a substitute for the real relationships the children craved and needed with their dads. For some fathers, giving presents was cheaper and more convenient than spending time with their children. It is no wonder that such people see prayer as bringing God their shopping list of current needs while having no interest in a relationship with Him.

When children are abused and violated by a cruel parent, as adults it is very hard for them to believe that God is not going to treat them in the same cruel and offhand way. At the very least, they often believe that He wants to use them for His own purposes.

When trying to understand the importance of prayer, we must begin by asking God to help us get a right perspective of who He is and what He is like. Jesus was obviously very aware of the problem, for on several occasions He told people that He and the Father were one. He said that if people got to know what He was like they would also know what the Father was like. In John 14:7 Jesus said, "If you really know me, you will know my Father as well."

I have prayed for many people. Often they have no problem relating to Jesus as God. But many of those same people have a real problem praying to God as Father. Jesus made it very clear that one of the reasons He came to live on earth was to show us what the Father is really like.

Putting Things Right with Father God

Before we move on I would like to ask you to spend some time thinking about how you see Father God. What does He seem like to you? Then think about how you saw your own human father. Ask yourself if you have believed that God the Father has some characteristics and habits that are not true to who He is. Are they a reflection of the distortion you may have experienced through the parenting you received?

Dealing with distortions to be able to really know God the Father is an easy process. First, speak out forgiveness to your dad (and maybe also to your mom) for everything that he did that gave you a wrong impression of what the Father God is really like. Tell God you are sorry for believing things about Him that are wrong and ask Him to forgive you. Thank Jesus for coming to show you what the Father God is really like. He is loving, kind, gentle, caring, compassionate, understanding and selfless. Finally, ask God to set you free from all of the false ideas that the father of lies (Satan) has sown into your mind and understanding since you were conceived and born.

Drawing on the enabling power of the Holy Spirit within you, start putting into practice what we have been talking about. Start living with a constant awareness of the presence of God. Start talking to Him as a friend. He is the very best Father there has ever been. Tell Him how much you love Him, share your thoughts, your visions, your dreams, your concerns, your feelings and your temptations. Tell Him about the bad or difficult things as well as the good and exciting things. He is interested in them all. This is prayer.

We take our dog for a walk every day. While I enjoy these times with Barney, they are also a very precious time of fellowship with Daddy God, which is what the Hebrew word *abba* means.

As I walk down the lanes and along the edge of a canal, I tell God about all of the things that are happening in my life. If you were to listen to my thoughts or hear my spoken words, you would not recognize them as prayers in the traditional sense. By that I mean the sort of prayers after which you would say "amen." They are, however, as legitimate as the most formal and carefully worded prayers you have ever heard.

It is simply me chatting with the Father God. Some people would think that was irreverent, but I do not think so. At the heart of these prayers is the simple recognition that Father God is the most important person in my life. I want to be involved with Him, and I want Him to be involved with me.

I often return having had a real time of fellowship with the Father and having heard Him speak to me as well. It is not surprising that on these walks I enjoy some of my most creative thinking. In fact, some of the best ideas I have ever had have popped suddenly into my mind at times like this. God is a Creator, and He loves us to be creative with Him.

Ready for More?

Now we are ready to move on in our understanding of prayer and look at what Jesus taught His disciples about prayer. This is important for us, because what mattered for the disciples of Jesus also matters to us.

SUMMARY

Prayer is much, much more than spending occasional times talking to God or repeating prayers. Prayer is the means of communication in the very special relationship that God longs to have with us. It is vital that we get a right understanding of what God is like, otherwise we will not be able to trust Him when we talk with Him.

PRAYER

Thank You, Father God, that You are interested in all of Your children, including me. Help me to always remember that no matter how I may feel, You do really care for me, and You want to have a relationship with me. In Jesus' name, Amen.

THE LORD'S PRAYER —WORSHIP AND ADORATION

"Our Father in heaven, hallowed be your name."
Matthew 6:9

We have now realized that prayer without relationship is definitely not what God intended. Indeed, we have seen that the very essence of prayer is the expression of an intimate relationship between Father God (Abba) and us (His children).

Children who love their daddy and have no fear of him have that glorious habit of interrupting the most serious of conversations with the simplest and seemingly unimportant comments, questions or requests. For children, their question is the whole of their world at that moment. They are oblivious to whatever other issues may be occupying their daddy's mind. And that is how it should be.

Daddy might be wrestling with major family or financial problems, struggling with his work or trying to work through some deep theological issues, but all his son or daughter wants to know is "Why are dandelions yellow?" or "Where is my teddy bear?"

The Lord's Prayer—Worship and Adoration

In a similar way, God may be watching in anguish as the nations rebel against Him and wars are about to break out across the world, but one of His children is praying for someone who is sick. Or another may be asking the Lord for help understanding His Word. Does God say He is too busy for such things? Of course not. He loves to hear and answer our prayers and relate to us as if we were the only person on the planet. I learned to talk with God in this sort of way as a child because I was used to hearing my dad and my grandfather talk to God like that.

That level of intimacy with God is not something that all people desire or feel comfortable with. To them it can seem dangerous to be letting God deep into their inner beings in such an informal way. If they want to pray at all, they seem happier with the security of more formal prayers. These prayers do not require any personal accountability or involvement with the God they are praying to, and people who are only able to pray in this way are missing something vital in a living relationship with God.

Please hear me carefully. I am not saying that formal, written prayers are unnecessary or wrong. I love some of the great prayers of the Church, prayers that Christians have been saying for hundreds of years that are full of profound truth. But if such prayers are not set in the framework of an intimate relationship with God, they can become the sort of dead routine for which Jesus criticized the Pharisees and religious leaders of His day.

Many of the psalms are based on the intimate relationship David had with his God. He interspersed freely his expressions of adoration and worship with the intimacy of his own spiritual experiences. The most well-known psalm of all, Psalm 23, is a wonderful example of how a man of God could talk naturally and personally about the Lord being his shepherd. There was nothing dead or formal about these words. They expressed David's personal experience of the God he knew and trusted so well. He was testifying to the reality and the nature of his relationship with God.

Take a few moments to read through those beautiful words of Psalm 23 and see how closely and intimately David had learned to walk with God. I am sure that David also used more formal words that had become

The Vital Breath of Prayer

part of prayer and worship in his day, but if those prayers were outside of a personal relationship with God, would they have had any meaning or been effective?

In Isaiah 1:15, God expressed His personal pain. Even though His people did all of the right things as prescribed in the Law of God, their hearts were far from Him. He even went so far as to say that He would not hear their prayers. It is obvious that an intimate relationship with His people really matters to God.

There was an occasion when Jesus was in the streets with His disciples and He saw people making a show of their public praying. These people would often perform their repetitive praying in places where everyone could see them—in the synagogues or on street corners. Jesus pointed them out to the disciples and called them hypocrites (see Matthew 6:5).

He said they already had their reward in full (the reward probably being pride and the feeling of how good they thought they were). This means that the prayers themselves were of no value whatsoever. They were of no benefit to themselves or to others. Then Jesus told the disciples that this was not the sort of praying in which He wanted them to engage. He said very firmly, "Do not be like them" (Matthew 6:8).

Jesus did not simply tell His disciples what they should not do. As a wise teacher, He also gave them a pattern to follow as they developed their own prayer relationship with God. We call it the Lord's Prayer.

How Jesus Taught His Disciples to Pray

This pattern for praying has been enshrined in the service books of almost every Christian denomination for the past two thousand years. More often than not, the Church has made use of it in a way that is exactly the opposite of what Jesus intended.

Jesus was trying to move the disciples away from repeating prayers as the hypocrites were doing. He wanted them to learn something entirely new—a pattern for guiding their prayer lives. It was to be an outline for praying that they could use in all of the circumstances of life.

The Lord's Prayer—Worship and Adoration

In calling this prayer the Lord's Prayer, we have got it slightly wrong. It was not a prayer that the Lord could pray in its entirety. Jesus had never sinned, but a section of the prayer shows us how to deal with sinfulness. It would be more accurate to call this wonderful prayer the Disciples' Prayer, for it is a prayer that Jesus intended His disciples throughout history to make their own. For our purposes we will continue to use the more familiar title of the Lord's Prayer now that we have understood for whom this prayer was intended.

If we use the prayer wisely it will become a life-changing daily experience. It will help us to walk confidently with God as we are aware of His presence and power in our lives. We will be looking at how to apply this prayer in our lives in the following four sections: Adoration and Worship, Kingdom Authority and Trust, Forgiveness, and Deliverance and Protection.

Adoration and Worship

"Our Father in heaven, hallowed be your name" (Matthew 6:9).
"Our Father, who art in heaven, hallowed be thy name" (Christian Tradition).

The first part of this pattern for prayer that Jesus wanted us all to use is about worship. It is about recognizing that God is our Father, that He is holy and that He is the source of everything.

In many ways our services and fellowship meetings have given us the wrong impression of what worship is supposed to be. People talk about having or attending worship, they ask who is leading the worship, or they say that we will have twenty minutes of worship. What people are talking about is singing Christian songs, which can be a very blessed and powerful part of our relationship with God. To think, however, that singing Christian songs is the sum total of worship is to miss the heart of what worship really is.

It is sometimes helpful to get a Hebraic insight into the things that we read about in the Bible. In Hebraic tradition, everything we do is seen as worship, and every breath we take contributes to a life of worship.

In living the life that God breathed into us, we are giving glory back to Him. In that manner, we are always worshiping.

This gives us a huge insight into how to live godly lives. If we look on everything we do as either an expression of worship to the God who gave us life (see Acts 17:28; Colossians 1:17) or to His enemy, Satan, then that perspective can act immediately as a brake on our temptation to sin. It is impossible to sin against God at the same time that we are truly worshiping Him.

If we recognize that every breath is both a gift from God and an act of worship, why would we want to waste our breath doing something that causes us suffering and that causes God grief and pain?

As we learn to love and adore God as the ultimate source of everything that is good, our attitudes in every area of our lives change, and our eyes are opened to see the whole of creation from a very different perspective.

Every day I look consciously at something God has made and marvel at the creative genius that lies behind this amazing world. That is a form of worship. Today I looked intently at the amazing camouflage pattern on the wings of a moth that strayed into our house. Tomorrow it might be the petals of a rose. And the day after that it could be a painting created by an artist using his or her God-ordained creative gifts.

Our Father

The first word of the Lord's Prayer is *our*. That is a plural word. We cannot pray this prayer and begin it with the words "my Father." God has created us for relationship. While God is the ultimate Father of every single one of us, He has also created us to be in relationship with each other. Jesus was drawing our attention to something very important. None of us is an island that is separated from the rest of humanity. God is Father to the whole human race. We are brothers and sisters with the whole of humanity.

In a family, brothers and sisters are defined as being the children of the same parents. And while there is always some friendly rivalry between brothers and sisters, they are united as siblings by a common and inseparable bond.

Even though my own brother and I were four years apart, we were very close to each other. We each knew that regardless of wherever in the world we were, if one of us was in need, our brotherly relationship and bonding would supersede every other situation. We were brothers, we loved each other and we mattered to each other.

By introducing this prayer, Jesus was saying that all of us in this human race are brothers and sisters because we all have the same Father. Even our enemies have the same heavenly Father that we do. God wants us to look on every other member of the human race as our brothers and sisters, people who matter to us.

In Heaven

There are many concepts in Scripture that are hard for us to understand. We read, for example, that we can never escape from God's presence (see Psalm 139:7–12). This means that there is nowhere I could go in all of creation where God is not present, even in this fallen, sinful world. At the same time, Jesus tells us that our Father is in heaven where there can never be any stain of sinfulness. There cannot be any overlap between the fallen sinfulness of the physical realms (over which man was given dominion) and the holiness of the heavenly realms in which God resides. Yet God is always there for us wherever we are, whether in heaven or on earth.

As a true Father, God is always there for His children. He is close enough to hear the faintest cry of the human heart while at the same time being able to reside in the holiness of heaven's eternal realm. Father God and Jesus the Son await the end of the ages when Jesus shall come again to reign on earth and then take His Church home to be with Him in heaven for eternity.

For now, I am content to appreciate the mystery from a distance, knowing that at the present time we are looking at these things as a poor reflection in a darkened mirror that one day will be made clear (see 1 Corinthians 13:12).

Hallowed Be Your Name

The very name of God is holy. In Jewish tradition the name is so holy that it is an offense to even print it on paper. Because of that, His name is never fully written down. We do not worship the name of God, but we do worship the God whose name is holy. We honor and respect His name. We worship Him by honoring His name not only by saying that we honor it, but by the way we live our lives.

Christians are representatives of the living God in this fallen world. We serve Jesus as the King of our lives. What we do, therefore, really matters. As the King's representatives, His name is written on our hearts. We belong to Him (see Jeremiah 31:33).

We are identifiable as citizens of the Kingdom of heaven. We may not wear a uniform as members of the Salvation Army do, but Scripture does urge us to be clothed in righteousness (see Romans 3:22; Isaiah 61:10; Ephesians 6:14). Righteousness should be the uniform of the disciples of Jesus. Charles Wesley expressed this thought perfectly in the final verse of his great hymn "And Can It Be, That I Should Gain," perhaps the most well-known of all Wesley's hymns:

> No condemnation now I dread;
> Jesus, and all in Him, is mine!
> Alive in Him, my living Head,
> And clothed in righteousness divine,
> Bold I approach th'eternal throne,
> And claim the crown, through Christ my own.*

If someone is wearing a uniform identifying himself as a member of a particular organization and commits some crime or does something morally indefensible, the individual will not only carry personal responsibility for what he does but also responsibility for damaging the name and reputation of the organization to which he belongs.

In the same way, when Jesus' representatives fall into sin, they not only have personal accountability for what they have done but they are

---

*Charles Wesley, "And Can it Be, That I Should Gain?," Hymnary.org, https://hymnary.org/text/and_can_it_be_that_i_should_gain.

also responsible for the shame that has been brought to the name of God and the Body of Christ. His name can be dishonored by our behavior.

Conversely, we honor and hallow the name of God when we choose to walk in holiness. Scripture puts it this way: "But just as he who called you is holy, so be holy in all you do" (1 Peter 1:15). We hallow His name by walking in holiness. Hallowing the name of God is a way of life. It is not just a group of words that are part of the Lord's Prayer. As we use the prayer, we ought to be thinking about whether or not our life is honoring to God.

Other Names of God

There are many other names used in Scripture to describe the nature and character of God. Names such as Jehovah-Jireh (God my Provider), Jehovah-Rapha (God my Healer), Jehovah-Rohi (God my Shepherd), Jehovah-Tsidkenu (God my Righteousness) and El-Shaddai (God Almighty). All of these are like different facets of a diamond. Each one gives a different insight into who God is. Each one sheds more light on the glory of God.

The more we learn about the nature and character of God, the more we will love Him and the more we will want to honor His name. We will not want to allow our behavior to discredit the organization to which we belong—the Church.

The Church is the family of God, the Body of Christ here on earth (see 1 Corinthians 12:27), the people of God who are called out of darkness into His glorious light (see 1 Peter 2:9).

And Finally

JOURNEY TO FREEDOM is not designed to give people more information. It is designed to be a series of practical steps that help you walk in the ways of God for the rest of your life. As a practical step forward, I encourage you to ask the Holy Spirit to shine the light of truth into any area of your life that could be seen as dishonoring to the name of God. When we are aware of a problem, we can do something about it.

SUMMARY

The prayer Jesus taught His disciples to pray was not meant to be repeated without understanding, but rather to be lived as a day-to-day experience of intimate relationship with the living God. We worship God and honor His name by choosing to walk in His ways because we love Him.

PRAYER

Lord, I thank You that I am a member of the most wonderful family in the world—the Body of Christ. I acknowledge You as my Lord and choose to honor Your name and to worship You through walking in obedience to Your call on my life for the rest of my days. In Jesus' name, Amen.

THE **LORD'S PRAYER—** **KINGDOM AUTHORITY** AND **TRUST**

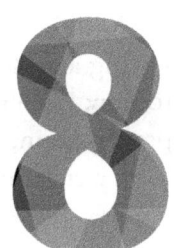

> "Your kingdom come, your will be done, on earth as it is in heaven. Give us today our daily bread."
>
> Matthew 6:10–11

I learned the Lord's Prayer as a child. On my bedroom wall was a wonderful picture of Jesus looking out over Jerusalem. I would often look at that picture and somehow in a childlike but confident way I truly knew that I could trust Jesus. He was not simply a picture on a wall; He was real, He was alive and He loved me.

At night I would kneel with my mother or father and say my prayers. Always, my simple prayers were concluded by us saying the Lord's Prayer together. I knew that this was what Jesus taught us to pray. The main prayers at almost every church service I ever went to were rounded up neatly by everyone saying the prayer that Jesus taught us. It did not matter whether the service was in an Anglican church, a Presbyterian church, a Baptist church, a Methodist church or a Brethren church.

The Lord's Prayer has entered into the spiritual culture of all of the traditional churches.

It was only in my teenage years that I stopped to think about what the words of the Lord's Prayer might actually mean. I read a wonderful book by G. A. Studdert Kennedy, who was an amazing army chaplain from World War I. He had learned how precious and important this prayer was while caring for soldiers in extreme life-and-death battle situations. In his book *The Wicket Gate*, he took people through his understanding of the various phrases of the prayer. It opened a window of heaven for me.

Until that time, I only knew the prayer as the Lord's Prayer without having any deeper understanding of how Jesus wanted the disciples to pray. Each time since then when I have been prompted to study the prayer again, I have realized that there is endless treasure to dig out from a rich mine of truth.

Your Kingdom Come

Albert Schweitzer, a missionary doctor who founded the world-famous Lambaréné hospital in Gabon (formerly French Equatorial Africa), said "There can be no Kingdom of God in the world, without the Kingdom of God being in our hearts."*

Schweitzer grasped a vital and foundational truth that determined how he spent his most remarkable life. Because man had been given authority by God over the world, it was through man only that God's Kingdom authority could be exercised on the earth.

The world, however, had become full of evil and the kingdom of darkness reigned because man's earthly authority had been given over to the evil one. As a result, the only way the Kingdom of God could now be established in the world was through the higher authority of the Kingdom of heaven being established in the hearts of the King's followers.

Wherever God's people are, the Kingdom of God is. This is exactly what Jesus meant when He said to some of His disciples, "Tell them, 'The kingdom of God has come near to you'" (Luke 10:9).

---

*Albert Schweitzer, *Albert Schweitzer's Ethical Vision: A Sourcebook*, ed. Predrag Cicovacki (Oxford: Oxford University Press, 2009), 73.

But what does this mean specifically in practical terms? When we look carefully at the four gospels, we discover that each one has a different emphasis. John's gospel, for example, is clearly the gospel of the evangelist. Matthew's gospel has always been known as the gospel of the Kingdom because it is full of references to the Kingdom of God or the Kingdom of heaven.

Jesus tells us in the Lord's Prayer that Father God lives in heaven, so it does not really matter if we talk about the Kingdom of God or the Kingdom of heaven. They both mean the Kingdom established by the living God that is administered from His home in heaven.

A kingdom is only a kingdom if it has a king. The king of the Kingdom of heaven is Jesus. The Bible refers to Him as the King of kings (see Revelation 17:14). Before Jesus began His work, John the Baptist, the last of the Old Testament prophets, told the people to "Repent, for the kingdom of heaven has come near" (Matthew 3:2). That meant that the King of heaven was about to begin His ministry on earth. And when Jesus began His teaching ministry, He used exactly the same words (see Matthew 4:17).

Throughout Matthew's gospel, Jesus tells many different parables, most of which begin with words such as, "The kingdom of heaven is like. . . ." In these parables Jesus used many different pictures to help His hearers discover the truth about God's Kingdom. Parables that began with phrases like "the kingdom of heaven is like a man who sowed good seed in his field" (Matthew 13:24) or "like a mustard seed" (Matthew 13:31) or "like treasure hidden in a field" (Matthew 13:44) or "like a merchant looking for fine pearls" (Matthew 13:45) or "like a net that was let down into the lake" (Matthew 13:47) or a number of other illustrations.

It is clear from these parables that the concept of the Kingdom of God was very important to Jesus. He wanted His followers to understand it. In Luke 9:1–2, Jesus sent His disciples out to do the same sort of work that He had been doing, and He told them to "proclaim the kingdom of God."

At the same time, He gave them His power and His authority to "drive out all demons and to cure diseases." There is a strong link between the disciples needing to have Jesus' power and authority and His instruction to preach the Kingdom of God.

Kingdom Praying

When the followers of Jesus pray the words *Your Kingdom come, on earth, as it is in heaven*, for what are they praying?

Some people think this is a prayer that is looking forward to the second coming of Jesus, when He will reign on planet earth for a thousand years (see Revelation 20:4). This is a period of time known as the Millennial Reign.

Such a prayer might sound something like this, *O Lord, things are so bad here on earth that we cannot survive much longer without You. We would love to see life on earth be like it is in heaven. Please, Lord, come again soon and set up Your Kingdom here on earth.*

The problem with such an interpretation of the prayer is that at the time Jesus gave the Lord's Prayer to His disciples, they had not even understood that Jesus was going to die on the cross and be raised again from the dead. They had not received any teaching about how Jesus would ascend to heaven and afterward would come again to earth. They were only at the beginning of their learning experience about eternal truths.

No, this is not a prayer about the Second Coming. Jesus intended it to be a prayer of immediate relevance and importance to His disciples. Jesus was also giving the Church for the whole of time an important pattern for their regular daily praying and living.

Jesus knew that one day soon He would be returning to heaven and that God had originally given authority (dominion) on planet earth to mankind (see Genesis 1:26–28). He knew that the only way the Kingdom of heaven could come on earth would be through men and women, as Albert Schweitzer had concluded accurately. The authority of the King of kings would first have to be established in their lives through relationship with Him.

Because Jesus delegated His power and authority to the disciples, they were able to do the works of Jesus, including giving commands to the demons. Whenever humans exercise the authority of Jesus over the works of darkness, they can also establish Kingdom authority on earth in the name of Jesus (see Matthew 16:19).

When Jesus told the disciples to tell people that the Kingdom of God had come near them, He was saying that whenever Kingdom authority is established, the Kingdom of God exists there and then. If we have invited Jesus to be Lord and King in our lives, then right here is where the Kingdom of God is. Wherever the reign of the King is established, the Kingdom of God is also established.

When Jesus is Lord of our families, our homes, our churches, our places of work, our businesses and even our nations, the Kingdom of God is established in these places. Within this Kingdom the disciples of the King will be at peace with God and with each other. Others will then have the opportunity to be introduced to the King and to enter the Kingdom of God for themselves.

This, however, cannot be regarded as a permanent state of affairs. The position of authority is maintained only when God's Kingdom people maintain their stands as disciples of Jesus. The god of this world will try to continually undermine them and win back the ground.

As a result of the Fall, we have to contend with weeds that grow up and pose a threat to the plants we want to nurture (see Genesis 3:17–18). No one has to plant those weeds, and unless we make an effort to remove them from our gardens, they will claim the territory back as their own very quickly.

In the same way, the enemy will claim back territory that mankind allows him to take. This happens if God's people move away from a place where they lived and worked formerly, if they give up the struggle for holiness and godly order in their lives or if they cease to exercise Kingdom authority in the places for which they are responsible. That is why there is much in Paul's epistles about the need for perseverance and endurance.

That is why we need to keep praying *Your Kingdom come* throughout our lives.

Over a hundred years ago the valleys of Wales were alive with the songs of believers. A revival was sweeping through their nation. Thousands of people were born again, hundreds of chapels were built and the glory of God came down. But there was little perseverance in discipling the believers and holding the ground that had been won for the Kingdom of God. A movement that bore amazing fruit in many other parts of the world, including Korea, died quickly back to virtually nothing in the place that gave it birth. The enemy had claimed back the ground.

What Does This Prayer Mean for Me?

When we pray *Your Kingdom come, Your will be done, on earth, as it is in heaven*, what we are really praying is this: *Lord, help me to live day by day, having the strength of will and purpose to choose to do your will in every area of my life. That way I know Your Kingdom will be established in my life and in everything for which I am responsible.*

This is not a passive prayer. After praying it we cannot sit back and wait for God to act. It is a very active prayer that requires our full participation in the ongoing will and purpose of God. No wonder Paul encouraged his readers to take every thought captive and make them obedient to Christ (see 2 Corinthians 10:5).

Paul knew that if our thought life could be brought under the Lordship of Jesus, then our actions would also be godly, and God's Kingdom purposes would become the norm for our lives. There is no doubt that if we choose to walk in godliness even though it may be hard, we may encounter the roaring lion that Peter describes the devil to be (see 1 Peter 5:8). But God will strengthen us by the power of His Spirit to do His will and to be overcomers.

Earlier I mentioned Albert Schweitzer. He was a great man, a great theologian, a great musician and a great physician. He could have had the world's adulation in any one of those career disciplines. He chose, instead, to be obedient to the will of God for his life (see Isaiah 58:7–12), and he sacrificed all of his time to build and run a mission hospital for the desperately poor and needy in West Africa.

There is no doubt that he knew the joy of seeing the Kingdom of God established on earth, and in his place of service he lived a very full life for more than ninety years. This is what he said to others who visited him: "I do not know what your destiny will be, but one thing I know: the only ones among you who will be really happy are those who have sought and found how to serve."*

It is in finding and doing the will of God for your life that you enter into your destiny and build God's Kingdom.

Let us pray: *Your Kingdom come—in all of my life and in everything I do.*

You may find it helpful to make a list of all of the different things that your life consists of, such as personal dreams and ambitions, home, family, relationships, private thoughts, hobbies and recreation, church life, work, finances, public life, etc., and then spend time bringing each of these areas before the Lord, asking if you have established His Kingdom authority in those places. This will give you clear guidelines for using the Lord's Prayer to initiate a life-transforming effect on everything you are and everything you do. Is that not what our journey is all about—letting God transform our lives from the inside out?

Trusting God for Our Daily Bread

"Give us today our daily bread" (Matthew 6:11).

In many of the things Jesus said, there is both a natural and a spiritual meaning. To understand this, we often need to look at different verses so that one verse can provide understanding about another. When the children of Israel were wandering in the desert and unable to farm the land, God fed them supernaturally every day (except on the Sabbath). He gave them manna, the bread of heaven, fresh on the ground daily (see Exodus 16:35). For forty years God did not forget the physical needs of His children.

In a similar way, Jesus provided bread and fish for the five thousand. He blessed a boy's five loaves and two fish, and as the disciples distributed the little in their hands they found that it multiplied as they gave it away. It multiplied so much that there were twelve baskets full of leftovers (see Luke 9:10–17).

---

*Albert Schweitzer, Pass It On, https://www.passiton.com/inspirational-quotes/7079-i-dont-know-what-your-destiny-will-be-but-one.

Everyone knows that physical bread is a basic food and is essential for physical life. But on other occasions, Jesus used the image of bread as a picture of the spiritual food that is also essential for daily life.

In John 6:35 He referred to Himself as the Bread of Life and said, "Whoever comes to me will never go hungry, and whoever believes in me will never be thirsty." When He was talking to the woman at the well, He said that "whoever drinks the water I give them will never thirst. Indeed, the water I give them will become in them a spring of water welling up to eternal life" (John 4:14).

In these passages Jesus is referring to the lifelong spiritual sustenance of our inner being. Without this we would never be able to be part of the answer to the previous part of the prayer, *Your Kingdom come*.

It is clear, therefore, that Jesus is concerned for both our physical and our spiritual needs. When He encourages His disciples to pray for their daily bread in the Lord's Prayer, He is referring to the supply of the essential basics of life, both physical and spiritual.

He is not referring to all of the things that we might want or might like to have. It is not wrong to want things beyond our basic needs; God gave us the whole world and everything in it to enjoy. But Jesus encourages us to trust Him and to cry out to Father God to show us how He can meet our needs.

The Divine Law of God's Provision

I believe that when we choose to walk in relationship with God in loving obedience with Jesus as our Lord, we will discover that there is a divine law in place. Whenever we draw on Jesus for the living bread and the water of life to meet our spiritual needs, the blessings that flow from our relationships with Him will overflow into the physical realm. We will then start to see God meet our physical needs in ways that may surprise us.

This principle is at the heart of the blessings promised to those who walk in obedience to the covenant provisions of a loving God found in Deuteronomy 28. When we walk forward with clean hearts, we are in the best place for God to bless the work of our hands. As a result, we will know His extraordinary provision for the Kingdom works for which we were made.

I can testify to the truth of this principle through personal experience. When I was in the business environment as a publisher and bookseller before the work of Ellel Ministries, the most profitable projects were always those that developed from ideas that arose supernaturally. Things would happen that were beyond the obvious. Ideas or dreams would come seemingly from nowhere. When I followed up on those supernatural ideas, it was as if God had gone before me and prepared the way. He is truly the best businessman.

The apostle Paul summed up his life of service to God with a statement of faith based on his experiences of God's provision: "And my God will meet all your needs according to the riches of his glory in Christ Jesus" (Philippians 4:19). Amen.

SUMMARY

Giving Jesus His rightful place as Lord of our lives is the most important step we can take toward ensuring that the Kingdom of God will be firmly established in and through everything we are and everything we do. God rejoices to meet our physical and spiritual needs daily as we choose to love and serve Him.

PRAYER

Lord, I want to walk in Your ways and do Your will in my life. Thank You for showing me that as I choose to make You Lord of each area of my life, this releases Your power, authority and provision into everything I do. That is how I want to live for You. In Jesus' name, Amen.

THE LORD'S PRAYER —FORGIVENESS

"And forgive us our debts, as we also have forgiven our debtors."
Matthew 6:12

"Forgive us our sins, for we also forgive everyone who sins against us."
Luke 11:4

"Forgive us our trespasses, as we forgive those who trespass against us."
Christian Tradition

You may like to take a deep breath before considering the next part of the Lord's Prayer. We all need to know that our sins have been forgiven by God, but in this prayer Jesus links the forgiveness of our own sins to whether or not we have also forgiven those who have sinned against us. For some people, this is a huge difficulty.

Taking That Deep Breath

In praying with thousands of people over many, many years of ministry, the largest single obstacle I have found to people knowing the healing and restoring power of God is their unforgiveness of others who have hurt them.

Do not worry that Luke's version of the Lord's Prayer refers to "Forgive us our sins," whereas Matthew's version says, "Forgive us our debts." The meaning is the same. Matthew makes it abundantly clear that Jesus emphasised the need to forgive others for their sins by saying: "For if you forgive other people when they sin against you, your heavenly Father will also forgive you. But if you do not forgive others their sins, your Father will not forgive your sins" (Matthew 6:14–15).

There you have it straight from the mouth of Jesus. If you do not forgive others, then God will not forgive you. Those are words that none of us really want to hear.

When other people have hurt us, we rise up instinctively in self-defense and justify our reactions with thoughts such as *They do not deserve to be forgiven.* And that is true. They do not deserve to be forgiven.

But, my friend, neither do you or I deserve to be forgiven. Forgiveness is not a matter of whether or not we deserve it. It is a matter of grace and mercy that is motivated by love.

But Jesus . . . You Do Not Understand . . . It Is Hard

It is easy to start arguing with Jesus about having to forgive others, and the arguments can seem sensible.

Just look at what they have done to me. Why should they get off? Why should I suffer for what they have done and then forgive them as if it does not matter? They have ruined my life. It is not fair. Surely, Lord, my situation is much worse than anyone else's.

But then our minds turn to that scene at Calvary. Jesus, the sinless Son of God, is being nailed to a wooden cross for something He did not do. From His lips come these words, "Father, forgive them, for they do not know what they are doing" (Luke 23:34). Our arguments melt away into insignificance when we think about what He did for us.

Recently I visited Rwanda in central Africa. In 1994 there was a terrible genocide with about a million Tutsi people being massacred by the Hutus. On this trip it was wonderful to spend time with people from both sides of that terrible conflict to see how God was rebuilding the nation through forgiveness and reconciliation.

One of the people who suffered greatly in the genocide was a fourteen-year-old girl named Rose. All of her family members were killed on the same day. Thinking that she was also dead, the villagers buried her with them. But, miraculously, the heavy blow to her head had not killed her. When she was dug out of the grave fourteen hours later, she was still alive. Her suffering was terrible.

A few years later, she became a Christian, and her life was transformed completely. It was as she read her Bible that she understood Jesus was asking her to forgive the people who had done these terrible things. The man who killed her father was now in prison, so she went to the jail to speak forgiveness to him.

It was this act of obedience to Jesus that opened the door to her healing. Twelve years after her terrible ordeal, as she was going through a nine-week training school at Ellel Grange, she was healed of the constant head pain and nightmares that had been a result of her terrible experience. Forgiveness opened the door to both healing and restoration.

Forgiveness did not change Rose's history, but it did change her future. It meant that Rose would be able to live the rest of her life without being in the chains of bondage that unforgiveness ties around many hearts.

It is not true to say that Jesus does not understand our situations. He not only understands, but He has also walked through the ultimate forgiveness test himself. He forgave those who were taking His life for something He had not done. Jesus helped Rose walk a similar pathway, and it is a journey that she will never regret.

I once prayed with a lady during a healing retreat who had been bitter for thirty years because of what cruel people had done to her. She had vowed never to forgive them. But the consequence for her was a deteriorating physical condition that was eating her life away. In the same way, bitterness was eating her heart away.

She wanted prayer for her physical condition, but forgiving those who had hurt her was not on her original agenda with God. She was quite angry when I taught her about the need to forgive. It was when she chose to forgive that the power of God was released into her life. She then received major physical healing for the condition that had previously crippled her.

Why Must I Forgive Others?

It is clear from the Lord's Prayer that for disciples of Jesus forgiveness has to be a way of life. It is not easy. Even Simon Peter struggled with the teaching and challenged Jesus with a question we could all have asked. "How many times shall I forgive my brother or sister who sins against me? Up to seven times?" (Matthew 18:21).

Jesus' reply must have shaken Simon Peter, for what he heard coming from Jesus' lips was, "Not seven times, but seventy-seven times" (Matthew 18:22). The Jews understood that this passage meant not to even start counting because there is no limit.

Jesus knew that if He set a certain number of times that we would have to forgive, we would store up all our venom and hatred and let it all out on, say, the eighth time. The fallen heart of man cannot be trusted.

Also, if there was a limit to the number of times that we have to forgive other people for what they do to us, then there could also be a limit on the number of times that God would forgive us. And that is something none of us would want to contemplate.

While the people who are forgiven will be blessed by our actions, the primary reason Jesus wanted us to forgive others was so that our own hearts would be free of the bondage into which unforgiveness locks us. We need to release people from the hook binding them to us and place them firmly into the Lord's hands for Him to deal with.

There is no doubt that unforgiveness and bitterness is a primary source of stress, pain and occasionally physical sickness. Even the medical profession recognizes this fact. Some doctors, for example, say that those who are bitter and unforgiving are more likely to suffer from conditions such as arthritis.

Forgiveness and Trust

I am sometimes asked whether or not forgiveness of others means I have to trust the people I have forgiven. The answer is a clear no. Once trust has been broken, it takes time for it to be restored again. The person who has harmed me needs to prove that it is safe for me to trust them again in the future. I need to know that I will be respected and not taken advantage of.

There are some areas of sin, such as sexual abuse, where offenders should never be trusted again with the lives of vulnerable people. This is for their own sake as well as for everybody else's. It is not right that through misplaced trust that they should ever be released back into a similar area of responsibility and temptation.

Forgiveness and Justice

Some people do not want to forgive because they see it as excusing the person from any responsibility and accountability for what they have done. But forgiveness has nothing whatsoever to do with escaping justice.

If a burglar broke into my house and stole things that were precious to me, I would be upset and angry, but I would forgive the person who did it. I would not want to remain in bondage to unforgiveness. Despite forgiving the person, I would still want the burglar brought to justice. He broke the law of the land and should pay the price for what he has done.

Forgiveness releases me from the consequences of bitterness. It does not release the burglar from the requirements of justice. I know some people who have found it too hard to forgive, especially those who have suffered the kind of terrible things that went on in places like Rwanda. They thought that if they forgave someone, it also meant they had to allow that person to escape the consequences of what they had done. That is not the case.

The sin of mankind separated the human race from a holy God. We inherited the death sentence. The death of Jesus on the cross was an outworking of justice. The price of death was paid, but by a sinless man who could not be held beneath the waters of death. Justice was required and justice was carried out. God's desire for us was to be forgiven and restored to a right relationship with Him; however, this did not mean that the requirements of justice could be avoided. God's Son, Jesus, made a way back to God for each of us who chooses to receive Him as our Savior.

Back to the Lord's Prayer

Why did Jesus include a commandment for us to forgive others inside of a prayer that asked God to forgive us? He was applying what is often referred to as the Golden Rule: "Do to others as you would have them do to you" (Luke 6:31).

We all want God to forgive us for the things we have done that are contrary to the Law of God. In the Golden Rule, Jesus is saying that if this is how you want God to treat you, then you need to be aware of the attitude of your own heart toward those who have sinned against you. The attitude of your heart determines whether or not God is able to answer that prayer.

The greatest blessing that any of us can ever experience is having our sins forgiven. Nothing releases the power of God into our lives more immediately or more effectively than receiving His forgiveness. The cleansing flow of forgiveness from the heart of God washes away our sin completely and makes healing possible in our lives. That flow of blessing starts when we forgive others.

When we forgive others, we are releasing them from our concern into the hands of God to whom we will all have to give an account. He is the only truly righteous and merciful judge.

Unforgiveness and the Need for Healing

Bitterness and unforgiveness have consequences. When we have unforgiveness toward someone, few of us stop to think about how deep and dangerous those consequences are, especially when they are tied to anger and a desire for revenge.

The Vital Breath of Prayer

These are Satan's weapons, and when we use them against others, they rebound on us. This process has the effect of opening a door to the work of the enemy in our lives. No wonder Paul warned us about not giving a foothold to the enemy (see Ephesians 4:27).

When the door of unforgiveness is left open, the consequences can spread much further than our feelings. Quite often our body begins to reflect the bitterness in our souls, and physical consequences are created. How do I know that? Because of the large number of people that I have seen get healed physically when they have chosen to forgive and have asked Jesus to set them free from all of the consequences of their unforgiveness.

I have met many people who have been abused, injured in accidents, accused unjustly, betrayed, taken into ungodly relationships or suffered the pain of rejection. Some were disabled, either physically or psychologically, some were victims of accidents and some were victims of other people's carelessness.

Most people came for prayer because of the symptoms they were experiencing, including everything from depression to major physical conditions. There was one pathway on their road to healing that none could avoid treading—the pathway of forgiveness. As they forgave those who had hurt them, the power of God to heal and deliver was released into their lives. Each personal story is a miracle of God's amazing grace.

I will never forget teaching on forgiveness at our first major conference in Hungary in June of 1991. During that very week, the last of the Russian occupying forces were leaving the country. The people had been so crushed by the loss of freedom and direct oppression from the occupying forces that many of them showed the signs of that crushing in their bodies, specifically in the way that they walked. As I looked at the hundreds of people present, my heart went out to them and I longed to see them released from their bondages. I longed to see them begin to walk tall again as a free people.

There was only one way forward. I knew I would be walking on sensitive ground when I talked to the people about choosing to forgive their Russian oppressors. They had all been brought up in the control of the communist system. Many had been treated very cruelly, much of their property had been stolen and their identity as human beings had been taken from them. Forgiving the Russians was not something they wanted to think about.

As I taught from the Word of God, however, it was clear that the people were understanding the message of the Lord's Prayer. If they wanted to truly know the release of God's love and power in their lives, they needed to express forgiveness for their Russian oppressors. Very tentatively I took them through a prayer of forgiveness, inviting them all to say the prayer with me in their own language. As I did so, I was praying that the Holy Spirit would begin to touch their lives. He did.

After they had all prayed, I then prayed for them. I asked that God would release them from the spiritual chains of oppression and set them free from the control of their spiritual enemy. I had no idea what would happen next. None of us could have anticipated how the power of God would come down on all those wonderful people.

Many were being delivered from the evil one. I then prayed for physical healing as our large ministry team mingled with the people. They prayed for healing for each person as they anointed them with oil.

It was a totally unforgettable sight. The Shepherd of the sheep was moving among His flock healing, delivering and restoring them. About 75 percent of those present confirmed that they had been healed of back problems. It was totally extraordinary. God was truly setting the captives free. Before our eyes we were seeing the fruit of what Jesus was teaching in the Lord's Prayer. What happened that day was miraculous.

Since then I have experienced many such days, either when teaching to a crowd or ministering to the needs of an individual. I now know from experience that Jesus knew exactly what He was doing when He included the need to forgive others within the framework of the Lord's Prayer.

What Should I Do?

In a practical way, we are now seeing why Jesus did not want us to repeat prayers without living them. We cannot pray the Lord's Prayer sincerely without being challenged about the need to forgive others. But it is only as we do it that we fulfill the conditions for our own forgiveness.

I know it is hard. To forgive others goes against the natural desire of the flesh. We discover the carnal nature when we choose to follow Jesus. It opposes everything godly in our lives just as the weeds in our garden oppose the growth of the plants and vegetables we are trying to nurture. The enemy does not want us to forgive, because that releases us from his control. Sometimes we feel able to make a choice to forgive in our minds and with our wills, but our emotions take a long time to catch up with our choices.

My strong recommendation would be that you spend a quiet moment thinking back through your life and really pray this section of the Lord's Prayer. Have a piece of paper handy and ask God to show you the names of all of the people who have hurt you in the past. Go back in your memory as far as you are able, even to early childhood.

Write down the names of everyone who has hurt you on your piece of paper. Some of you may come up with quite a list. Take those names one by one and think about what was done. Ask God to help you by the enabling power of His Holy Spirit to speak out your forgiveness. Then, again by the enabling power of the Holy Spirit, release each person on your list into the freedom of your forgiveness. Ask Jesus to set you free from the consequences of unforgiveness that have been in your life. You will be amazed at what God begins to do in your life as He lifts the burden that the enemy has put upon you.

Once you have brought your forgiveness up to date, then perhaps at the end of each day you could think back over the previous 24 hours and speak out your forgiveness to anyone who has offended you.

Keeping our hearts clean like this on a daily basis is a precious discipline that will always equip us for living the life of a disciple of Jesus Christ.

More Reading

You can read much more about the importance of forgiveness in my book *Forgiveness—God's Master Key* available on the Sovereign World website at www.sovereignworld.com.

SUMMARY

Jesus linked the forgiveness of our own sins to our willingness to forgive others. If we do not forgive those who have hurt us, then we lock ourselves in a prison of our own making. Turning the key of forgiveness is the only way out of the jail.

PRAYER

Thank You, Jesus, for dying on the cross for me so that I might be forgiven. Help me to forgive all of those in my past who have hurt me. Help me to keep my forgiveness of others up to date on a daily basis so that I may never again be in bondage to the enemy through unforgiveness. In Jesus' name, Amen.

THE LORD'S PRAYER —CRYING OUT TO GOD

"And lead us not into temptation, but deliver us from the evil one."

Matthew 6:13 NIV

"And lead us not into temptation, but deliver us from evil: For thine is the kingdom, and the power, and the glory, for ever. Amen."

Matthew 6:13 KJV

The traditional King James Version of this amazing prayer ends with a glorious statement of truth. It underlines everything that has gone before about Kingdom authority and the fact that every single thing we know of on this planet has its source in the presence and the glory of God.

We must not let the absence of this statement from some modern translations of the Bible rob us of the joy of affirming the glorious truth of the Gospel.

A Cry from the Depths

Before we reach the glorious climax to the traditional prayer, there is an extremely important petition that cries out to God from the very depths of fallen humanity. It is a cry that keeps us in touch with the spiritual reality of living in a fallen world. It is a world that has Satan as its god till Jesus comes again (see 2 Corinthians 4:4).

As we have now established together, there is an unending war on for the souls of men, and temptation is the primary weapon Satan uses to seduce us from the highway of holiness (see Isaiah 35:8).

For God to be true to Himself, He cannot encourage us to walk in righteousness without also wanting to protect us from wrong choices that would lead us into unrighteousness. Therein lies God's dilemma. He has given us free will. For us to enjoy His protection, we must want to have it and ask Him for it. Otherwise God would have to go against our free will in providing us with His protection. To do that would be contrary to His creative order for the human race.

If we did not have free will, we could not have a relationship of love with our Creator. But having free will puts us in constant danger of succumbing to temptation and grieving the God who loves us so much. This is the reason that we need to desire constantly the Lord's protection from the wiles of the evil one. We need it for ourselves and for those God has placed under our direct covering for spiritual protection. This would apply especially to our children and our children's children.

Psalm 91 speaks of the shelter and protection that God wants His children to enjoy, but the fulfillment of those wonderful promises is incumbent on us choosing to dwell in the shelter of the Most High (see Psalm 91:1). The promises do not apply to those who want to live outside the covering of God. This indicates clearly that we have to take an active role in securing God's protection for our lives. If we do our part, then God is able to do His part.

Does God Tempt Us to Sin?

The phrase "lead us not into temptation" that is found in the Lord's Prayer might be interpreted to mean that God could be the source of temptation. This is clearly one of those statements from Scripture where we need clarification from another Scripture verse.

We find the answer in James 1:13: "When tempted, no one should say, 'God is tempting me.' For God cannot be tempted by evil, nor does he tempt anyone."

Nothing could be clearer than this statement. The above verse might even have been written by James to clear up questions people were asking about the meaning of the Lord's Prayer. God can never be the source of temptation. What then does this phrase about temptation from the Lord's Prayer actually mean?

Let us read the next verse from James: "But each person is tempted when they are dragged away by their own evil desire and enticed" (1:14).

Temptation is enticement from the enemy to do those things that arise from the evil desires that are inherent in our fallen, carnal natures. That is not God's heart desire. He can never be the source of either the evil desire for sin (from a carnal nature) or the enticement (the temptation that comes from the evil one).

What Does the Prayer Mean?

Let me answer this question with a story from my own experience. When I was nineteen I sailed alone around Africa. I wanted to explore my own heritage and roots from that most amazing continent. With some money left to me by Ouma, my South African grandmother, I bought a ticket on a ship of the Union Castle Line. I was an innocent young man with all of the normal desires of the flesh, and I could have been quite vulnerable to a variety of temptations.

I know my parents were praying for me, probably harder than I realized. Saying the Lord's Prayer was part of my own daily devotions. While the desires of my flesh might have been saying one thing, I had no desire in my spirit to succumb to ungodly temptations that I knew I would regret for the rest of my days.

I boarded my ship, the *Stirling Castle*, at Southampton, fully aware that life on board an ocean liner was full of potential temptations. I was to share a cabin with two other men, but I had no idea who they would be. I was first in the cabin and took the top bunk. The next guy came shortly after that. Just before sailing time, the door of the cabin was pushed slowly open by our third companion, a very elderly man.

I looked down from my top bunk and was both shocked and pleased when he looked up at me and revealed the clerical collar around his neck. I was shocked because I knew instantly that the very presence of this man would be a godly check on all that I might have wanted to do on the ship. In my spirit I was rejoicing that I was to share the cabin with a fellow believer. God was answering my prayer.

His name was Rev. Dr. Ennals, and he was 95 years old. Even though 76 years divided us, we had a unity that transcended age. The following Sunday morning, just south of the Bay of Biscay, Dr. Ennals led an evangelistic service on the deck of the ship. I joined him by playing the piano for the service. God had ensured that my personal colors were now nailed carefully to the mast of the Gospel throughout that thirteen-day voyage.

There were several hundred passengers on board, but Rev. Dr. Ennals was, to my knowledge, the only clergyman on the ship. I am certain that whoever was responsible for making the cabin assignments was guided by the hand of God. The prayer *Lead us not into temptation* had been answered remarkably. Whether that was an answer to my parents' or my own prayers, I will never know, but I did know that there was no way that I could let the temptations of the flesh overcome the choices of the spirit during that voyage. God was in charge of my life.

For me, the meaning of this vital phrase from the Lord's Prayer is two-fold:

> First: *Lord, please do not lead me along pathways where the temptations will be so strong that I will not be able to resist them.*
>
> Second: *Lord, please go ahead of me as my shield and protector so that when I do face temptation, I will be strong enough to resist the devil in whatever form his temptations may take.*

For these prayers to be an effective expansion of the prayer *Lead us not into temptation*, they have to be the desire of our hearts. There is no point in praying the prayer with our lips while having a completely different intent in our hearts.

The essence of God's answer to these prayers is summed up in a wonderful promise from the book of Proverbs: "He holds success in store for the upright, he is a shield to those whose walk is blameless, for he guards the course of the just and protects the way of his faithful ones" (2:7–8).

But What about Testing?

After Jesus was baptized by John the Baptist and filled afresh with the Holy Spirit, Scripture tells us that He "was led by the Spirit into the wilderness to be tempted by the devil" (Matthew 4:1). Could that not mean that when people are tempted by the devil, it has been organized for us by the Holy Spirit? And if that is so, how could Jesus encourage us to pray *Lead us not into temptation* when it seems as though behind our backs the Holy Spirit and the devil are laying traps for us?

This is an important question that we need to answer. In some ways every single temptation we face is a test. The enemy tests us to the limit, always looking for a gap in our defenses that he can exploit. The testing Jesus experienced when the Spirit of God led Him into the wilderness was testing of a different nature and of a different magnitude.

As is clear in the story of Job, this sort of testing is allowed and is even encouraged by the Holy Spirit. It takes place when men or women know that God has called them, and their resolve to follow that calling is being tested.

This kind of testing is not simply a trap of the enemy to tempt you to sin. It is a specific onslaught on your calling that God allows for your own good and your own strengthening. You may not like it, but it is vital that we are tested before a work of God begins.

Having read the personal stories of many Christian pioneers and having shared hearts with leaders across the world, it seems that this sort of experience is far more common than is appreciated.

The Lord's Prayer—Crying Out to God

The following is an account of my own personal experience in this respect.

Shortly after God gave me the vision for the work of Ellel Ministries, I experienced a night of spiritual terror. The vision was burning in my heart, and I knew that this was what God had made me for. I was pressing joyfully on with thinking and dreaming about the work when on this particular night it seemed as though God left me. I discovered something of what it was like to be in the spiritual realms but without the Spirit of God. It was a lonely and very frightening nighttime experience.

It was my own long, dark night of the soul that culminated in what felt like a personal visitation from Satan. Whether or not it was Satan, I will probably never know, but it felt as though it was. I was wrestling with an evil being, and I knew that I did not have the resources to win the fight.

I knew also that there was only one issue at stake in this spiritual battle—the vision that burned within me. I knew that if I agreed to give up the vision, the devil would leave me, and the battle would be over. But I knew also that if I gave up the vision, I would spend the rest of my days heartbroken that I had not done what God had called me to do. I could never give up the vision, and I was reiterating this constantly to the enemy as the battle raged.

Throughout this terrible experience, every part of my being was involved. My whole body was covered in the sweat of battle. I do not know how long the battle went on, but there came a moment when I was aware once again of the presence of God. I was able to call out to Him again. Immediately the devil left me. He was unable to hold any ground in the presence of God. That night I believe the Lord allowed the devil to test my calling.

I have often thought about that evening, especially in times of great hardship and pressure. It has given me great encouragement to know that there is nothing the enemy can do that can stand in the presence of the Lord. He is sufficient for every crisis and every need. I can even thank God now for that time of testing, because over the years it has often been a comfort to my soul to realize that He was really with me.

We need to be on our guard constantly against the many other temptations (testings) of the enemy. He will target all our soulish desires and seek to divert us from the path of holiness. Let us not flee from those times of testing that the Spirit of God prepares for us. They are to strengthen us and encourage us for the future.

It is really great to know and see proof of the truth of 1 Corinthians 10:13:

> No temptation has overtaken you except what is common to mankind. And God is faithful; he will not let you be tempted beyond what you can bear. But when you are tempted, he will also provide a way out so that you can endure it.

Deliver Us from the Evil One

Sometimes people say to me that believers should never need deliverance. They believe that no born-again believer can ever be affected by the presence of an unclean spirit or a demon. Then why did Jesus encourage us to pray for deliverance from the evil one? "And lead us not into temptation, but deliver us from the evil one" (Matthew 6:13).

We need deliverance from the evil one in two ways. We need deliverance that is the protection of God. It comes from Him, and it keeps us safe from attacks of the enemy as we walk in obedience to Him. But we may also need the deliverance ministry that Jesus did constantly throughout His ministry on earth as He fulfilled the prophecy of Isaiah 61:1 and set the captives free by casting out demons.

We will learn much more about this later on when we look specifically at the work of deliverance as part of God's healing provision for His Church.

To God Be the Glory

"For thine is the kingdom, and the power, and the glory, for ever" (Matthew 6:13 KJV).

What fantastic truth brings this wonderful prayer to a close. If this was the only sentence of the Lord's Prayer that we really got hold of and lived its meaning all our days, it would transform our lives completely.

More about Prayer

In these few sections about prayer and praying, it has only been possible to look at the vital foundations for a godly prayer life. This publication focuses on what Jesus stressed as being of primary importance for His disciples.

There are many other aspects to prayer that are also important, such as waiting on God, listening to God, praising God in all circumstances, intercession for others, spiritual warfare and thanksgiving. But if we do not have the foundations in place, these other aspects of prayer will be in danger of only being words. Instead, they should be an expression of a prayer relationship between the heart of man and the heart of God.

SUMMARY

We have seen how God wants each one of us to live in such close fellowship with Him that prayer as conversation with God becomes a way of life. Prayer was never intended by God to be something that was an activity of the human spirit isolated from the rest of our humanity. The whole of our being needs to be involved in our relationship with Him. We should never lose sight of the fact that God is everywhere and that wherever we are, we are in God. That is where the Kingdom of God is. The Lord's Prayer, or the Disciples' Prayer as I called it, provides us with a wonderful pattern to use as the basis for all our praying. It embraces worship, submission to God's Kingdom authority, confession, repentance of sin, forgiveness, intercession for our needs and prayers for protection from all of the attacks of the enemy. Adapting this pattern into a daily discipline for prayer is a dynamic and life-changing experience. It is a brilliant foundation for the daily transformation that God will bring to you on our journey to freedom.

PRAYER

Lord, teach me to pray. Show me how to use the Disciples' Prayer as a foundation for my daily praying. Keep me, Lord, from all of the traps that the evil one may lay for my life. I not only want to begin my life of discipleship well, I want to finish it well, too. Thank You for the promises of protection in Your Word for those who choose to walk the highway of holiness. In Jesus' name, Amen.

STAGE 5

HEALED FOR A PURPOSE

God's purpose for my life is more important to me than anything else on the planet.

WHAT DOES HEALING MEAN?

Now that we have completed the first four stages of our journey to freedom, we are starting to look at some of the practical consequences of the things we have been learning. We will also go back briefly over some of the topics that we have already looked at to study them in greater depth than was possible during the introductory stages of our journey.

Back in 1970 when I looked at the bent and broken chassis of my old car, God used the Alvis Speed 20 to point me in the direction He had for my life. When God told me that I could restore this broken car but that He could restore broken lives, He certainly got my attention. Through this experience He began to show me His purpose for the rest of my days.

It was no surprise to me that I had more to learn on this topic. God placed me in many situations that would teach me what He wanted me to learn about healing. I discovered that healing was definitely on God's agenda for His Church today.

But I also discovered how much work God had to do in me so that I could be ready and equipped for the work He had for me to do. I had much to learn, and not all of the lessons were easy ones. I made mistakes. I realized, though, that often I learned more through the mistakes than I did through anything else. I also learned that God does not reject me because I make mistakes. I did realize, however, that if I did not learn from the mistakes, I would have to keep on taking the same test time and time again.

My Own Journey

Since becoming a believer at the age of nine, I have been aware that calling and destiny are important to every single believer. It is our responsibility to passionately strive to walk in the ways of the Lord. We all have a purpose to live for. Nobody is without value or purpose in the Kingdom of God.

In the churches of my youth and young adulthood, healing was not taught from the pulpit. Reaching out to people outside the church with the Good News of the Gospel was encouraged, but developing a healing ministry to people inside the church was unknown.

It seemed to me that once people were saved, they were expected to play their parts as members of the various organizations within the fellowship, to contribute to the offerings and to get ready to take their places in the congregation of heaven.

Even though the Lord's Prayer was said at every single service, the whole concept of seeing His Kingdom come on earth as a realistic hope seemed very far from the expectations of the leadership.

Healing ministry was not on the agenda of the leadership. If someone was either physically or psychologically sick, the appropriate solution was to send them to the doctor and then pray for them to get better. This was done from a distance. While I thank God for doctors, they cannot give pills that will treat the human spirit or that will heal the root causes of the conditions of the soul. Some medication can help people cope with symptoms while they are struggling for survival, but there is a huge difference between treating symptoms and healing the root of the problem.

Often the only time people received personal prayer was when they were ill. Their names would be read out during the Communion service, and a prayer would be said for their healing. But the idea that there could ever be a link between a person's illness and their spiritual condition was, seemingly, an unknown truth.

What Does Healing Mean?

Deep down I was unhappy with this. During my college days, I tried to break out of this theological mold without even realizing I was in it. Somehow, I knew that God had answers that no one was giving me. I started going with a team of young ministers-in-training at Wycliffe Hall Theological College in Oxford to conduct ward services at local hospitals or at an institution for young offenders. I learned to play the piano accordion to provide some musical accompaniment so that I could relate to these very damaged young people. I was groping in the dark.

Several times a day on my college campus of Christ Church, I would pass between the portraits of the great evangelist John Wesley and the great children's author Lewis Carroll (pseudonym of Rev. Charles Lutwidge Dodgson). John Wesley had been instrumental in changing the spiritual landscape of England in the eighteenth century. An evangelical revival swept the country under his leadership. Lewis Carroll changed the face of children's writing in the nineteenth century with his amazingly imaginative writings about Alice in Wonderland.

Both Wesley and Carroll had been students at my college and were an inspiration to me. Like John Wesley, I have never lost the love of seeing someone come to faith in Christ. And I still love reading the creative writing of people like Lewis Carroll. As great as Wesley and Carroll were, they did not provide the answers I was looking for (although I now understand from many of Wesley's writings that he did understand the need for healing in many of the people who came to faith through his preaching).

While at Oxford, I cast my eyes up and down the theological spectrum, went to all sorts of meetings and tried to help many people in different ways, largely without success. I left Oxford eventually with a degree in chemistry but with more questions than answers about the issues of life that really mattered and about what my own personal calling before God would be.

Broken Lives and Broken Hearts

I was 26 years of age when I stood looking at the wreck of that Alvis Speed 20 and God spoke to me about broken lives and broken hearts.

It was as if I knew what I had been looking for. I could not articulate it theologically with chapter and verse from the Word of God, but I knew that what I was sensing was not from me. It fit all of the things I had been looking for during those years of searching.

As I looked at that car with its bent and broken chassis, I knew that unless someone took the time to dismantle, lovingly and carefully, every single part of the vehicle to find out what was wrong with each piece, and then carefully reassemble the parts in accordance with the maker's instructions, that this whole vehicle would be destined for the scrap heap.

In earlier years I had spent many hours in scrapyards looking for precious bits of motor that would help me keep another vehicle running. There was not much wrong with many of those cars in the scrapyard. Most of them had been abandoned by people who did not love them enough to care. Their owners had been attracted by the latest model in the showroom.

It did not take a great deal of imagination for my mind to wander from the picture of a field full of broken-down, unwanted motor cars to seeing some of the people in a congregation of Christians. I saw in my mind that many were going through the motions of going to church, singing hymns, putting money in the offering plate, listening to sermons and going home again. For those people it was much like sitting in a field of broken-down cars, wondering when the wrecker would come and crush them to bits.

Just like the car in my garage, these people needed someone to love and rescue them. No amount of praying for my old Alvis would change anything. I had to get my hands dirty while I worked. In much the same way, no amount of praying from a distance for the people whose lives had been damaged would do anything more than prop them up. In that condition they would remain unhealed and broken-down.

When I heard the voice of God say to me, *I can restore broken lives*, my heart leapt within me. I still loved the wreck of that old Alvis and saw its potential, but a greater love of seeing God restore broken lives took its place. Nearly forty years have passed. There is still a lot of work left to do on the car—one day it might be finished—but of much

What Does Healing Mean?

greater importance and value are the thousands of lives that God has touched since then.

According to the Maker's Instructions

The only way I could restore the bent chassis of the car was to obtain a blueprint (the engineer's original drawing) of exactly how the steel frame of the car should be. I wrote to the manufacturers. Amazingly, a few weeks later I was sent a copy of the chassis design blueprint. Immediately I could see exactly what had happened in the accident. More importantly, however, I could now see what work had to be done in order to restore the chassis to its original dimension.

Everything was distorted and had to be put back in order before it would be possible to start the work of restoring all the mechanical parts of the vehicle, putting them back on the chassis and preparing for the rebuilding of the body. While I still had many years of work ahead of me, the most important and helpful information was found in the maker's instructions.

It became very obvious to me that the reason why so many people were ineffective as members of the Kingdom of God and could only go through the motions of living a religious life was that the foundations of their lives (their spiritual chassis) had been distorted. They were trying to live while their lives were in a state of disorder. No amount of prayer for healing of the external symptoms and problems could ever be effective because the very foundations of their lives were out of line with God's best for them.

The original maker's instructions were absolutely critical to the restoration of the chassis in the Alvis. And in exactly the same way, our Maker's instructions according to His Word are equally critical to the restoration of broken lives.

Jesus used parables to teach the people eternal truths. In my own life, God has also used parables to teach me many things. The parables are often about things I am naturally interested in, such as old cars. It is exciting to look for those pictorial lessons that Jesus will use to teach us about how to walk in His ways.

A Definition of Healing

I am often asked about what Christian healing actually is. Sometimes people see you teaching about healing and then expect you to come down off the platform and start performing miracles. For some, the miracles of Jesus are the only frame of reference that they have for a healing ministry.

While there are times when I have seen God do extraordinary things that others might describe as miraculous, in almost every case it has been in response to the person choosing to get their spiritual foundations into godly order. To use the above illustration one more time, to get their chassis straightened.

The definition of healing that I am most comfortable with and the one that fits most accurately with Scripture from Genesis to Revelation is the restoration of God's order in a person's life.

This covers simply everything. It covers those who are struggling with a physical illness. Their body is out of order. It covers those who are wrestling with the pain of forgiving others for what they have done. It covers those who have been traumatized through abuse or accidents. It covers those who do not want to face up to the reality of unconfessed and unforgiven sin in their lives. It covers those who have entered into wrong relationships and are struggling with the consequences of sexual sin. It covers these and many more things. It covers everything.

The Story of King David

King David was an amazing man of God who had learned to trust and obey God from a very early age. This was the man who killed Goliath and became the hero of his people. But David also had a weakness. At one stage of David's life everything got quite out of order (see 2 Samuel 11 and 12).

As king he should have been away with his army at war. But he stayed at home and fell into the temptation of lust when he saw a beautiful woman (Bathsheba) bathing. He summoned her to his palace and committed adultery with her. She became pregnant.

He tried to cover up the consequences of his sin. He summoned Bathsheba's husband, Uriah, back from the battle and tried to persuade him to go home and sleep with his wife so that the baby would appear to be his. But Uriah felt that it would be disloyal to his country do so. David then arranged for Uriah to be at the center of an unwise and dangerous military operation. Uriah was killed.

This left the way clear for David to marry Bathsheba so that people would think that she had had an early delivery when the baby was born. Everything David did was designed to get himself out of trouble. In reality, however, every step took him deeper and deeper into the consequences of his original sin. Sin can only be hidden from view by further deception and more sin.

Finally, God broke this cycle of sin and deception by sending the prophet Nathan to confront David with his sin. David confessed, and everything he had done was brought into the floodlight of exposure. There was critical disorder in David's life.

David's actions broke the seventh commandment and were outright sin (see Exodus 20:14); however, this sin was not David's only problem. When David described in Psalm 51 how he had been feeling, he described himself as being sick. His bones ached and he had lost his joy (see verse 8), he could not stop thinking about what he had done and was probably losing sleep (see verse 3), he felt dirty and in need of cleansing (see verse 2), he was aware of the inner lies that he had used to try to defend his integrity with falsehood (see verse 6), he felt impure in his heart and he had lost his steadfast determination to be God's man (see verse 10). Worst of all, perhaps, was that he was living in fear that the Holy Spirit (who had been on him since his anointing for kingship) would be withdrawn from him (see 1 Samuel 16:13). What a mess David had gotten himself into.

It is obvious that David was now very sick and in need of healing. It is equally obvious that if Nathan had not come with the convicting word of the Lord, David's life would have gone downhill pretty fast. If this story had happened today, he might have started looking into counseling for his damaged emotions, medication for undiagnosed aches and pains, sleeping pills to cover the night hours and probably a referral to a psychologist or a psychiatrist for treatment of his depression.

There are many situations, especially for victims of violence and abuse, when the services of a psychologist or a psychiatrist have helped provide a way for people to reach a place of stability. That stability helped them to be able to face their real healing need.

But in King David's case, he did not need any of these treatments for the manifold conditions from which he was now suffering. What he needed was the restoration of God's order in his life. This could only come through confession and repentance followed by forgiveness and restoration.

I am using David's story as an illustration of how people can be in need of healing. They might not be sick in the traditional medical sense, but they are still desperately ill. Even in our churches there are many people who have wrestled with unconfessed sin for years and years. For some, the battle to keep it all in has become too great, and they have collapsed under the strain. In doing so they have succumbed to a range of possible sicknesses and conditions.

Others are not like David, but they are struggling with the pain of sexual abuse that occurred in their early years, the consequences of which are still devastating their lives thirty or forty years later. I will never forget praying with an eighty-one-year-old lady who shared for the very first time about sexual abuse that had happened to her when she was fourteen.

She had never revealed the secret because she mistakenly felt that she had a moral obligation to respect the reputation of the uncle who had done the damage. The abuse caused her to fear men, so she had never dared risk developing a relationship that might have led to marriage. What devastation she had been forced to endure.

The joy she entered into when she was able to finally talk it all out, forgive her uncle and then receive deep inner healing and deliverance was amazing. I knew that the joy of the Lord and His great love for her would be her strength in her latter days in a way that could never have been possible previously.

Restoring God's Order

As we work through these things together, we will see how the restoration of God's order in the foundations of our lives is critical to seeing God's power to heal and restore released into the rest of our lives.

A couple went through our Modular School doing one course a month over a two-year period. They began the school with a catalogue of issues in their lives. But as the school progressed, they dealt with their issues one by one. As they gave God first place in every area of their lives, the transformation was amazing. He brought His order out of their chaos. It is easy to love such a miracle-working God.

Satan uses the parts of our pasts that are unhealed to control our lives in the present and to rob us of our future destiny (see John 10:10). God does not want you to be healed just so that you will feel better, as wonderful as that is. He wants you to know the blessing of a life fulfilled, of living in the security of His Kingdom and of rejoicing in His love. As you apply the lessons of JOURNEY TO FREEDOM into your own life, you will see God changing you from the inside out.

SUMMARY

In order to establish God's healing in your life, you need to give God permission to rebuild the foundations according to the Maker's instructions. Then you can believe Him not only to heal you but also to restore your destiny and give you His purpose to live for.

PRAYER

Lord, thank You that You want to rebuild my life. Help me to walk with You through every area so that little by little You can put things right. I want to walk in Your ways and enjoy Your presence forever. In Jesus' name, Amen.

WHY DO I NEED HEALING?

Surely all we need is the Gospel and to know that we are born again. Is that not sufficient? When we get to heaven we will not have any problems, and there will be no more crying or tears (see Revelation 21:4).

Yes, that is the wonderful truth of the Gospel, but it does not deal with the time from when we were born again to the end of our lives when we get to finally be with God. We are living in that period of time. We cannot live in either the past or the future. It is possible for us to live in the present only, one moment at a time. We are always in the present moment, and that is the only moment that matters.

Why Do I Need Healing?

You might want to also add to this question ". . . especially when I do not think I am sick."

The whole of the Bible was written by the Holy Spirit to be a constant source of inspiration and encouragement for the people who are alive. That means you and me. There is nothing in the Bible to indicate that God wants us to remain in the state that we were in when we were first born again.

Why Do I Need Healing?

Even the apostle Paul was still pushing forward toward the end of his life. "But one thing I do: Forgetting what is behind and straining toward what is ahead, I press on toward the goal to win the prize for which God has called me heavenward in Christ Jesus" (Philippians 3:13–14).

The Christian life is a pilgrimage with a purpose. We are to build our lives on God's Kingdom principles, seek to avoid all the traps of the enemy, reach out to others who are not yet part of the family of God and minister the healing love of God to the hurting members of His family.

If we are going to minister His love to others, we must first choose to receive His love for ourselves and allow Him to have His way in our lives. It is that process that I refer to as healing.

I read a news report recently about a famous painting that had been vandalized. The person who defaced this priceless work of art with meaningless splodges of paint had been caught. His sentence gave him plenty of time in prison to think about what he did, and he is paying his debt to society.

Putting the man in prison, however, was not going to solve the problem for the art gallery. The damaged painting was still hanging on the wall. The answer for the painting was to bring in specialist restorers. It would take months of painstaking work for them to remove every trace of the modern paint and restore the surface of the original painting so that no evidence would remain of the damage done.

The prison sentence was dealing with the man's sin while the art restorers were bringing healing to the classic painting. Dealing with one without the other would not have been satisfactory.

Remember that our primary definition of healing is the restoration of God's order in a person's life. If we apply this principle to the painting scenario, the restoration of order required the detailed attention of the restorer to the area that had been damaged. God as our Restorer wants to give detailed attention to any areas of damage that we have experienced in our lives.

Satan is like a vandal who tries to destroy the image of God in the lives of God's creation. The sins of men are his only weapons, because it is only to man that God has given authority on this earth. Satan might be the instigator of evil ideas, but it is man who is the perpetrator. Satan may have been the one behind the horrific ideas of Adolf Hitler to exterminate the Jews, but Satan could do nothing without Hitler having been his agent and the perpetrator of those terrible crimes.

The Process of Healing

When the apostle John described in very simple terms how the consequences of sin should be dealt with (see 1 John 1:9), he said three things must happen for full restoration to take place. He described a process:

> First: If we confess our sins
> Second: God is faithful and just and will forgive us our sins
> Third: He will cleanse us from all unrighteousness.

John is very clear. Sin damages not only your relationship with God, which then needs restoring through forgiveness, but it also causes damage in you that needs cleansing. You need to be healed of the consequences of the sin.

Later we will be looking in much more detail at some of the consequences of breaking God's covenant. When you read through Deuteronomy 28 and see all of the physical consequences of sinful behavior, it is easy to understand why sinners not only need to be forgiven but also need to be healed. If they are not healed, then both the short- and the long-term consequences are serious.

The need for healing is not restricted to us. There are also secondary consequences of sin that affect everything that is under our spiritual authority, including families and land. They all need healing. This principle is implied clearly in one of the most well-known healing promises in the Old Testament. It is when God speaks directly to Solomon in response to his prayer at the dedication of the temple in Jerusalem.

This is what God said:

> If my people, who are called by my name, will humble themselves and pray and seek my face and turn from their wicked ways, then will I hear from heaven, and I will forgive their sin and will heal their land.
>
> 2 Chronicles 7:14

This is a wonderful and amazing promise. It spells out so clearly that not only do people need forgiveness for their sins, but they also need healing—and that healing extends to the land, meaning everything under a person's spiritual authority that has been affected by the consequences of their sins.

Sin and Sickness

In the New Testament the apostle Paul picks up on this vital teaching about the relationship between sin and sickness. In his instructions to the church at Corinth about how they should remember the death of Jesus at the Lord's Supper, he urges people to examine themselves carefully before taking the bread and the wine (see 1 Corinthians 11:28).

In many of our historic church traditions, which go way back to the very earliest days of the Church, it was normal for people to remind themselves of what all of the Ten Commandments said before making a general confession of their sins. Only then did they feel able to receive the bread and the wine.

The churches of the Outer Hebrides of Scotland still take several days to prepare the hearts of the people for the sacramental act of Holy Communion. It would be considered a grave sin not to examine one's heart most carefully and deal with all known sin before receiving the elements of the sacrament—and that needs time.

Paul explains why this sort of confession is important. It is not only that people need to know they are forgiven of their sin—which they do—but that if they act presumptuously and take the bread and the wine as if their hearts are right with God when they are not, then the personal consequences can be serious.

Paul explained it like this: "Whoever eats the bread or drinks the cup of the Lord in an unworthy manner will be guilty of sinning against the body and blood of the Lord" (1 Corinthians 11:27). It would be like invoking a curse upon oneself through entering into personal deception in the process of taking Communion. Whenever we cooperate in deception, it gives the enemy a foothold into our lives. This is serious stuff.

Then in verses 29 and 30, Paul explains further that men behaving in this way bring "judgment on themselves." As a result, "That is why many among you are weak and sick, and a number of you have fallen asleep." Paul was under no illusion that unresolved sin in anyone's life has a way of manifesting itself in sickness or death.

In 2 Chronicles 16:11–14, we learn that Asa, who was the king, developed a disease in his feet and eventually died. He died because of his sin of depending on a foreign and idolatrous king instead of trusting in God. We saw how David was beginning to suffer a string of related symptoms as a result of his adultery. Then in Proverbs 3:7–8, we read, "Fear the LORD and shun evil. This will bring health to your body and nourishment to your bones." The converse is that unresolved sin can have an unwelcome outworking in our lives.

It seems pretty clear that throughout Scripture we are discovering the same message. Sin does more than damage our relationships with God. It can also have a consequence of sickness in our lives of that needs healing.

It is as if there are three dimensions to the consequences of sin. One dimension is the damage that is done to our relationships with God. The second is the damage that may be done to our relationships with others—especially those we have sinned against. The third dimension is the consequential damage to us and to those who are under our spiritual authority.

Paul uses a picture from agriculture to illustrate his point. He says, "God cannot be mocked. A man reaps what he sows. Whoever sows to please their flesh, from the flesh will reap destruction" (Galatians 6:7–8). Paul says it so clearly that it is hard to understand how people cannot see his point.

To answer the original question in our title: Yes, we do all need healing because we are all sinners. We are living in a fallen world and none of us has escaped. When we get to chapter 25, we will learn what confessing sin really means. It is more than telling God what we have done wrong.

But Does That Mean That All My Sickness Is Caused Directly by Sin?

Yes and no.

Yes, in that if man had not sinned, everything would still be perfect and in the unfallen state. Satan would have no authority on earth, and there would be no sickness and no disease.

No, in that there are many sicknesses and diseases that are now endemic in the world, meaning that they are rampant across the planet and anyone can get them. They have become part of the human condition. We all suffer accidents and injuries of varying sorts. As a young man, I broke my nose on three occasions while playing field hockey and rugby. Such injuries are not related to sin.

While I was ministering in Rwanda, I was careful to take my antimalarial pills. If I had not taken the pills and I contracted malaria from a malaria-carrying mosquito, I would have been very angry with myself for not taking the pills. But I would not have thought that because I had sinned a mosquito came to get me. The connection between my malaria and sin would only be a very loose connection. Neither do I conclude that when I catch a cold that it is a direct consequence of my personal sin. It is not.

But if someone visited a prostitute who was HIV positive and as a result they contracted AIDS, there would be a direct link between their sin and the disease they now had. No wonder Proverbs tells us that avoiding evil is health to one's body.

What about Other People's Sin?

It now seems clear that we can be affected by the consequences of our own sin. What happens when other people do things that hurt us? Can that also cause us to need healing?

The answer to this question is a definite yes. Dealing with our own sin is only one side of the issue. Much of the time we also have to deal with the consequences of what others have done to us. It is not for nothing that Satan is referred to in Scripture as a thief and a robber (see John 10:10).

When people suffer as a result of their own ungodly choices, you could say they are only getting what they asked for. But when people suffer because of what others have done to them, the cruelty of Satan and the horror of sin become much more apparent. People are being robbed by Satan of their potential in God. Sometimes they are even being robbed of life itself.

It grieves God greatly to see people suffering unfairly because of what others have done to them. I believe that is why Jesus placed such emphasis in the Lord's Prayer on choosing to forgive others for what they have done to us. It is only then that we can escape the unfair punishment that Satan loves to load on us. Sadly, the very existence of sin in the world has guaranteed that life is not fair and that some people will suffer more than others.

There is only one place in the world where everything is seen to be fair for every human being. That is at the foot of the cross. We have all sinned, we all need forgiveness and there are no favors or preferences given. It does not matter whether or not one is a king or a penniless orphan. We are all at the same level resolving the question of eternal destiny before our wonderful Savior. It is where we receive forgiveness for the sin that separates us from a loving and holy God (see Romans 3:23).

The equality and fairness that was handed out to men and women at Calvary was made possible by the eternal unfairness of what was happening to Jesus. At the cross, the consequences of all of humanity's sin were loaded on the only person to ever walk this planet who did not deserve any of what He was suffering (see Isaiah 53).

What Must I Do to Be Saved?

It was in Philippi that the jailer cried out to his prisoners after the earthquake, "'What must I do to be saved?' They [Paul and Silas] replied, 'Believe in the Lord Jesus, and you will be saved—you and your household'" (Acts 16:30–31).

This was a wonderful answer to the eternal question of a sinner under conviction. But in the Greek of the New Testament, the words that are used for *being saved* and *being healed* are similar. How they are translated depends on the context of the passage.

Salvation and healing have the same source. It is the finished work of Jesus on the cross. Isaiah saw this very clearly when he prophesied that both salvation and healing would flow from the death of the sacrificial Lamb of God: "He was pierced for our transgressions, he was crushed for our iniquities; the punishment that brought us peace was on him, and by his wounds we are healed" (Isaiah 53:5).

Isaiah's prophecy shows clearly that both salvation and healing flow from the completed work of the Messiah.

To receive salvation, we receive Him as our Savior. To receive healing, we need the cleansing that the Savior can bring. "If we confess our sins, he is faithful and just and will forgive us our sins and purify us from all unrighteousness" (1 John 1:9).

In the next few chapters, we will be looking at how you and I can rejoice not only in our salvation, but also experience the Savior being our Healer.

SUMMARY

While all sickness and disease are caused by sin, not everything you struggle with in life is a consequence of your sin. The fruit of what Jesus did for you on the cross is seen in both your salvation (restoration of relationship between God and man) and your healing (the restoration of God's order in each one of our lives). Jesus died for both.

PRAYER

Thank You, Lord, for enduring the terrible unfairness of the cross so that there would be total fairness for every single human being who looks to You for salvation and healing. Help me during this week to be really honest with myself as I continue to walk a personal pilgrimage of hope, healing and restoration. In Jesus' name, Amen.

GENERATIONAL ISSUES

None of us arrived on the planet without a family history. Every single human being has been parented through many, many generations. When you were conceived, the generational history of your father through his sperm and the generational history of your mother through her egg combined to give you an inheritance that has influenced every area of your being.

The Bible pays a lot of attention to generational lines, giving detailed records of families. Sometimes it explains how one generation was affected by another. This is a subject that matters to God.

Down the Family Line

We have already established that you consist of spirit, soul and body (see 1 Thessalonians 5:23). We will be returning to look at what this means in more detail in a later section of JOURNEY TO FREEDOM, but for now we need to recognize that when God breathed His life into your human spirit at conception (see Genesis 2:7), the living soul and physical body that exploded into being carried with them a picture of your generational history. This is something that is seen and understood in the physical realm on the genetic level. The physical similarity of your genes to those of your parents and siblings confirms who you are related to and to which family you belong.

A few years ago, I stood in the Huguenot Memorial Museum in South Africa looking at pictures of some of my distant French ancestors who had established a new life in that far-off land. My wife almost burst out laughing as she looked from me to them and back to me again. It was very, very obvious that I was related to them by how much I resembled them.

No one could have doubted that I was a Huguenot who had descended from the de Villiers family line. I also recognized that I did not just carry the visual looks of those amazing people. Something of that same Christian determination was evident in my own life and was driving me on in the vision that God had given me for the ministry.

I remember praying for a lady regarding some unsavory aspects of her character that she was not proud of. She looked at me somewhat pathetically and said "Well, we Robinsons are always like this. Both my father and my grandfather were just like me."

She seemed resigned to a belief that there was no point in me praying for her because this was how all Robinsons were and nothing could be changed.

In English we say "like father, like son," which means that the son is taking after his father, especially in terms of character, gifts and abilities. We all know of people, possibly even in our own families, who bear a striking resemblance in looks, character or giftings to their mother, father, grandmother or grandfather. I have a friend who plays the flute brilliantly. His father was a great musician who founded an orchestra. He carries the blessing of that generational gifting.

Everyone has both strengths and weaknesses in their character or personality. It is not unusual to see the same strengths and the same weaknesses appearing one generation after another down the family line.

A man stood talking to me in the entrance hall at Ellel Grange. He was holding the hand of his six-year-old son as he confided in me why he had come for personal help. He said, "I have committed adultery, and my father before me and my grandfather before him. They all committed adultery."

He then looked from his son to me and back to his son again and asked a very poignant question. "What hope is there for him? I do not want him to walk in the same footsteps that I have walked in."

I was able to give him great encouragement as I explained how Jesus came to set the captives free. I shared that at that moment, he and his whole family line were in captivity to the enemy's control. He would have to make some choices and deal with the real issues, but if he was willing to walk God's way then both he and his son could be free forever of this curse on their family line.

At this point I need to explain what I mean, so let us go back to the Word of God and see what the Bible says about this critical issue.

The Sins of the Fathers

The Ten Commandments are described in Deuteronomy 4:13 as God's covenant. God's covenant does not refer to an agreement that was made between God and man. It is His gracious provision for mankind that arises out of His nature of love. The terms of God's covenant can never be up for discussion. They can only be accepted or ignored. They cannot be changed.

If God's covenant is accepted and is used as the foundation for life, then it will always be a source of God's blessing and loving protection (see Deuteronomy 28:1–14). If the covenant is ignored or rejected, then man has to live with the consequences of making choices based on spiritual ignorance, rebellion or moving outside of the boundaries of God's protection (see Deuteronomy 28:15–68).

We will be looking at the issues of covenant much more closely at a later date, but for now it is vital that we understand that the content of the Ten Commandments is as unchangeable as the law of gravity. We may not like the law of gravity, but as we have already seen, if we ignore it we will always suffer the consequences.

You cannot walk off the edge of a cliff without experiencing the effects of gravity. If the world would realize that the Ten Commandments

Generational Issues

are as certain and as unchangeable as gravity, people would then be far more determined to live their lives within God's boundaries without feeling they were being restricted or without feeling that God did not understand their situations.

Jesus said nothing that would undermine the importance of the Ten Commandments. He even went so far as to say that not one word of the Law would pass away until the end of all things and that whoever practices and teaches the commandments would be great in the Kingdom of heaven (see Matthew 5:17–20). When speaking to the rich young ruler, Jesus told him, "If you want to enter life, keep the commandments" (Matthew 19:17).

When the Pharisees asked Jesus which of the commandments was the greatest (see Matthew 22:36), Jesus did not quote one of the Ten Commandments. He instead gave them two principles: Love the Lord your God with all of your heart and soul and mind, and love your neighbor as yourself (see Matthew 22:37–39). He was not saying that the old commandments were redundant and that these were replacing them, but rather that these two principles summed up and embraced everything that is found within the Ten Commandments.

In fact, what Jesus said was that "all the Law and the Prophets hang on these two commandments" (Matthew 22:40). He meant that if we love the Lord our God and love others as ourselves, we would never want to do things that would take us outside of the provisions of the Ten Commandments.

The reason I am taking the time to show that the Ten Commandments is stressed in both the Old and the New Testaments is that some Christians seem to have developed a lack of respect for the commandments of God. They seem to regard them as mere history. Some have even replaced them with a model of conduct based on a selfish interpretation of love that has become a serious distortion of truth.

As a result, we have Christians who are quite happy to share in faith and worship with believers in Buddhism, Hinduism or Islam as if these religions worship the same God on an equal footing. We have people who have tried to rewrite the seventh commandment, "You shall not commit adultery," to fit in with their personal sexual desires and relationships. We cannot rewrite Scripture to suit ourselves (see Deuteronomy 4:2; Deuteronomy 12:32; Proverbs 30:5–6; Revelation 22:18–19) and think there will be no consequences. As Paul said to the Galatians, "God cannot be mocked" (Galatians 6:7).

The Ten Commandments are as important today as they ever were. They are a reflection of the unchangeable nature of God. The fundamental laws of science, which describe the behavior of the physical universe, cannot ever be changed because they are a reflection of the nature of matter itself. In the same way, the fundamental laws of the spiritual universe (the Ten Commandments, God's covenant) cannot ever be changed.

We may think that the commandments were all swept away with the New Covenant when Jesus came, but they are unchangeable truths. They are for our good. The Ten Commandments could be seen as the first handbook for successful human living.

Visited on the Children

Having now established firmly that the Ten Commandments are relevant for the whole of mankind for the whole of time, I want to draw your attention to one very important detail of great significance to our study.

> "For I, the LORD your God, am a jealous God, punishing the children for the sin of the parents to the third and fourth generation of those who hate me, but showing love to a thousand generations of those who love me and keep my commandments."
>
> Exodus 20:5–6

Because of the controversy that can exist around the translation of the first part of this verse, I want to tell you how the King James and the New American Standard Versions of the Bible translate the phrase *punishing the children for the sins of the fathers*. They both say "visiting the iniquity of the fathers upon the children."

The difference may seem small, but the impact of this difference is huge. Both Ezekiel and Jeremiah are clear in what they have to say. Ezekiel says that when it comes to punishment for sin, the sour grapes that the fathers have eaten will not set the children's teeth on edge (see Ezekiel 18:2). He also says that the son "will not die for his father's sin; he will surely live" (Ezekiel 18:17). As Jeremiah puts it, "Everyone will die for their own sin" (Jeremiah 31:30).

It is clear to me in the context of both of these passages that the sort of death being talked about is not the physical death that we will all experience, but rather the punishment of eternal death to the soul. I believe it would be unfair and unjust if God were to punish someone eternally for someone else's sin for which they were not responsible.

Even though it may not be personal punishment for someone else's sin, we cannot escape the fact that countless millions of people do suffer the consequences of another person's sin. In every single family, the children are inheritors of the consequences of the sins of their ancestors.

This is why the translation of this verse is important. The consequences of the sins of the fathers are visited on the children for at least three or four generations. But *visiting on* and *punishment for* is not the same thing.

In the book of Nehemiah, we read how Nehemiah is a prisoner of war because his ancestors had sinned (see Nehemiah 1). Lamentations 5:7 expresses it this way: "Our ancestors sinned, but now they are gone, and we are suffering for their sins" (GNT). This is reality.

We all know of people who have suffered the consequences of what their parents or distant ancestors have done. Maybe we have even suffered in this way. But suffering as a consequence of the sins of our ancestors is not the same as being punished by God for their sins.

A letter came recently to Ellel Grange from a lady who was asking for help. She explained how her former drug-addict husband had used every bit of his income to feed his habit rather than feed his family, and now their daughter was suffering under the consequences of his sin.

A baby born to a prostitute mother out of a casual sexual relationship with an alcoholic man will suffer the consequences of the lack of godly parenting. The child may well be far more prone to committing his own similar sins because of the spiritual influence of the ancestors and his learned behavior from one generation to another.

These are facts that we cannot ignore. The sins of the fathers are visited on the children—and, yes, it could take three or four generations before the consequences of ungodliness are eliminated from the generational line.

Conversely, however, a child born to a godly heritage will inherit and enjoy the fruit of all that is good and godly in the generational line. The spiritual blessings, the education and the example coming from one generation to the next can have dramatic and lifelong effects on the children of such a generational line.

There is a comparative study of the generational lines of two American families. They look at the godly heritage passed to the descendants of the great evangelist Jonathan Edwards and Max Juke, a man who did not know the Lord and lived a pretty ungodly lifestyle. These men were contemporaries. This is a summary of the report:

> The study included 1,200 of Max Juke's descendants and nearly 1,400 descendants of Jonathan and Sarah Edwards. Max Juke's descendants included over 200 convicts, 7 murderers, 190 prostitutes, and 440 alcoholics. Jonathan Edwards' descendants included 100 clergymen, 130 lawyers and judges, 65 college professors, 13 university presidents, 60 physicians, 75 military officers, 80 public office holders, 3 senators and 1 vice-president.*

This extraordinary comparison illustrates graphically how God has created humanity so that His blessings can come down the generational line. But individuals in each generation still have to make their own choices of how to live.

The fact that a generational line may be blessed by the Spirit of God does not guarantee that each generation will choose to walk in that blessing. God will never violate His gift of free will to mankind, even to make them good. People have a right to choose to either accept or

---

*Larry Ballard, "Multigenerational Legacies—The Story of Jonathan Edwards," YWAM Family Ministries, July 1, 2017, www.ywam-fmi.org/news/multigenerational-legacies-the-story-of-jonathan-edwards/.

reject God no matter how godly their generational line might be. We all have the free will to choose to sin or not to sin. Having a difficult ancestry does not mean we have no choice about sinning. It may be more difficult to make the right choice, but we still have a choice.

One of the consequences of mankind choosing to come under Satan's authority at the Fall was that everything God had created within humanity that was intended to be a blessing could now be used by Satan for his purposes. The capacity for blessing to flow down the generational lines could now be used by Satan to transmit cursing. As a result, demonic power that entered into a generational line through the sins of an ancestor could pass down that generational line from one generation to another.

I usually illustrate this by likening this generational spiritual link to a drainpipe on the side of a building. All the drainpipe has to do is transmit whatever liquid is poured in at the top. The drainpipe has no capacity to reject dirty water and to choose to transmit only clean water. It is simply a channel linking the top and the bottom of the pipe.

In the same way, the link from one generation to another cannot choose what sort of spiritual power it gets to transmit. It passes on whatever is poured in. This includes both the good and the bad.

If God were to make it impossible for evil demonic power to pass down that generational drainpipe, then He would have to block off the drainpipe altogether so that neither good nor bad could be transmitted. That would mean that whatever good was in our ancestral line would be denied to us.

When it says in the Ten Commandments that the sins of the fathers will be visited on the children, it means that whatever the family line has suffered as a result of the sins of the fathers will be a spiritual inheritance for the next generation. This is not God punishing one generation for the sins of another. But it is true that what we are and what we do does not stop with us. We pass it on.

If parents reject the covenant of God and His Word and take their family into sin, the children will suffer the consequences, often for several generations. Whether or not this is fair is not the issue. Sin is in the world, and the consequences of sin can affect many generations.

So What Can I Do? Is There Any Hope?

Yes, there is hope, and yes, there is something you can do. You can acknowledge the facts of your personal situation and ask God to remove the consequences of your past to establish a new generational line for your future.

Key lessons are found in the book of Nehemiah. In chapter 1, Nehemiah confesses that both he and his ancestors have sinned (see verses 6–7). None of us can repent for what others have done—their sin is their responsibility—but we can confess our ancestors' sins. We can agree that they have sinned, and then we can speak out our confessions and ask God to set us free from the consequences of their sins. We can then take authority over any unclean spirits that have been using the sins of our ancestors as a vehicle for transmitting their presence and influence from one generation to another.

After Nehemiah had rebuilt the wall, the people rediscovered what God's Word said. They "confessed their sins and the sins of their ancestors" (Nehemiah 9:2). They were dealing with the things they had done and also dealing with what their ancestors had done.

Both steps were vital so that the people could be free to serve God unimpeded by the spiritual consequences of their generational past. That is the place where I believe God would want us.

Dealing with the past in this way does not change history. It does not restore to you everything that the enemy has stolen. But what it does do is draw a firm spiritual line under the past so that you are free to start with a new and solid foundation to your life. As a child of God, you are an inheritor of all of the blessings that are Jesus' (see Ephesians 1:3–14). This includes His robe of righteousness, which is His family disposition. He writes His law in our minds and hearts (see Jeremiah 31:33), and His Holy Spirit enables us to walk in His ways. As a member of the family of God, you can start building a new and godly generational line to be a blessing to your children and your children's children.

This was the good news I was able to bring to the man standing in the entrance hall of Ellel Grange with his six-year-old son.

Under the New Covenant, the authority that Jesus had over the powers of darkness was delegated to His disciples. Now is the time to start living in the fruit of what Jesus did for us on the cross and to start saying no to the enemy and yes to Jesus.

My relationship with God should be the most important thing in the world to me. After that, His purpose for my life is more important than anything else on the planet.

Once we get our relationships with Him right, we can then start to move into the detailed purposes of God for our lives. Satan does not want us to know where he has a controlling influence in our lives, but God wants to expose his tactics for what they are and to see His children fulfill their destinies.

SUMMARY

We are influenced by both the good and the bad of the generations that have gone before us. We can thank God for the good, and we can deal with the bad as we confess what our ancestors have done. We can then forgive and release them into the freedom of our forgiveness. We can deal with the control of the enemy in our lives and start walking toward living in the freedom of the inheritance Jesus won for us on the cross.

PRAYER

Thank You, Jesus, that Your death on the cross was sufficient to deal with the consequences of my sin. Thank You that You want to set me free from the ungodly generational influences on my family lines. Help me, Lord, to put down a new foundation of truth in my life so that I may be a blessing to others. In Jesus' name, Amen.

THINGS THAT HAVE HAPPENED TO ME

I pray you are encouraged when you realize that not only does God have a real purpose for your life, but that He is also determined to help you clean up the past so that you can look forward to your future. It is out of having a relationship with Him that we grow into living a purposeful life for Him.

Because we live in a fallen world, nothing we experience this side of eternity will ever be perfect—other than, of course, the Lord Jesus. Paul rejoiced to say to his readers in Ephesus that He has "blessed us in the heavenly realms with every spiritual blessing in Christ. For he chose us in him before the creation of the world to be holy and blameless in his sight" (Ephesians 1:3–4).

None of us know from personal experience what it will be like to be totally holy and blameless. That is a joy that awaits us in heaven. But one of the many miracles of our salvation is that even at this present time when Father God looks upon us, He first sees the perfection of His Son. Our only means of access to the Father is through the Son. Seventy-two times Paul describes a Christian as being "in Christ." If we are in Him, then we are clothed by Him. His perfection is our clothing, even now.

The clothing that is Christ surrounds a life that has not yet been made perfect. It is a life that Paul also described in other terms when he said, "Not that I have already obtained all this, or have already arrived at my goal, but I press on to take hold of that for which Christ Jesus took hold of me" (Philippians 3:12).

In reality, we are people with carnal natures and damaged pasts who are en route to eternal citizenship in a Kingdom that we do not deserve to live in. Yet by God's grace we will. In the meantime, we strive toward this perfection from a position of faith and hope.

Jesus Said, "Come, Follow Me"

I often have the privilege of praying for people and listening to the stories of what has happened in their lives when I am at meetings and conferences. Becoming a Christian has given people a living hope for eternity, but the cry of their hearts is to see something made manifest in their lives of God's Kingdom life and dynamic authority now. When I hear the pain and the cruelty that some have suffered, or the depths of sin that people have either committed or been victims of, I marvel all the more at the wonder of the cross.

Yes, one day all the dross of this world will fall away. Praise God, you will enter into your eternal destiny. But first you have a destiny to fulfill on earth.

Yet there are many who will be trapped by their circumstances and will never see what they dream of and long for. At times like this, I can weep at the devastation in the lives of so many of God's children. I long to see the Body of Christ rise up in compassion and mercy going after the lost sheep and ministering hope to the family of God.

We have already seen that Satan is a destiny robber (see John 10:10). He wants to use every possible hook in our lives to prevent us from realizing our potential as citizens of the Kingdom of God. He wants us to look at the mess and to give up trying, which is the very opposite of what Paul was urging us to do when he said for us "to take hold of that for which Christ Jesus took hold of me" (Philippians 3:12).

Christ Jesus took hold of us because He loves us. He has a purpose for our lives (see Jeremiah 29:11; Ephesians 2:10), and right now He wants us to lift up our eyes and see beyond the limitations imposed by

Satan's horizons. Satan, however, wants to tell us that because of our personal failures, God will never be able to use us. Satan will always want to remind us of all of the limitations on our lives because of what others have done to us and because of what we have done. Satan will always want us to look backward and downward.

Jesus, however, says to look forward and upward. He called the disciples to follow Him at the beginning of His ministry (see John 1:35–43). He used the same words to call Simon Peter to serve Him after he had received deep, personal ministry (see John 21:22). This was when the call to follow Jesus touched the very core of who Simon Peter was and God's potential in him was unlocked.

From that moment on, the healed Simon Peter was a different man. In stark contrast to the fear that had gripped him when the servant girl questioned him, he proclaimed the glorious truths of the Gospel with a loud voice on the Day of Pentecost.

So many folks hear and respond to the first call to follow Jesus, but they never get to the place of receiving the healing we all need. They struggle to hear God calling them lovingly to follow Him into the place of service as a child of the King.

Journey to Freedom is about getting to that place in God where He can use us in His service for the rest of our days. I pray that this is the place where you want to be. I pray that as we share these precious days together, you are looking forward to the personal transformation He has for you.

Out of the Slough of Despond

In John Bunyan's amazing book *Pilgrim's Progress*, one of Christian's early experiences was trying to cross a dangerous piece of wet and muddy ground. It was a deep mire where he could have sunk easily. There seemed nowhere firm to place his feet, and the situation seemed hopeless. This mire was called the Slough of Despond. It was a place filled with fears, doubts and discouragement. There is a Slough of Despond today where Satan tries to do everything he can to push you under the mud. His goal is that you are never able to move forward in your pilgrimage.

Things That Have Happened to Me

We are going to take a hard look at ourselves to see how God wants to lift us out of the Slough of Despond.

I want you to ask yourself, "Is there anything that has happened to me in my past that is acting like a control or a brake on my future growth in God?"

We have already seen how we can be affected by the generational influences that have come down our ancestral lines. Later we will be looking at what we might have done that has given the enemy rights over our lives. We will examine things that Satan can still use to hold us in his control and bondage.

We are now going to look at some of the things that might have come against you throughout your life. We will start with the moment that you were first conceived and began your journey toward birth. Then we will continue our process examining the years of your life to this present moment.

Facing My Past

In Jonathan Swift's wonderful book *Gulliver's Travels*, Gulliver visits a place called Lilliput where all the people are very small in comparison to Gulliver's seemingly huge size. To the Lilliputians, Gulliver is a giant who could do terrible damage in their country. They have to take action to save their people.

They wait for Gulliver to fall asleep and then tie him down with their strongest ropes. To Gulliver, the ropes were thinner than the finest strands of cotton. He could have broken any of the individual ropes with a flick of his little finger. With hundreds of these ropes in place, however, he was bound securely enough that he was unable to move. He was a prisoner to a people who were no threat to him, but because they had bound him with hundreds of thin strands, the cumulative amount was too strong for Gulliver to break.

That is a very good picture of how Satan operates in our lives. Very few of the things that happen to us are strong enough by themselves to control us, but the combined effect of many things can hold us in bondage. The good news is that there is nothing that has happened to us in the past that Jesus cannot set us free from in the present. We have to play our part in the process. Salvation puts us into a restored relationship with God, but it is healing that releases us from the chains of bondage.

Here are some of the possible events in a person's life that if left unhealed could be used by the enemy to hold them back from their restoration and potential:

- Being unloved and unwanted by your parents.
- Being the wrong gender as far as your parents were concerned.
- Having siblings who were preferred above you.
- Never having had your interests, gifts and abilities recognized or encouraged.
- Being squeezed into a parental mold into which you did not fit.
- Being a victim of cruelty or abuse, sexual or otherwise.
- Being bullied at school or later in life.
- Suffering debilitating sicknesses, especially when you were young.
- Having accidents or traumas that caused serious personal suffering.
- Losing a parent or other close family member or friend when you were young.
- Suffering deprivation through poverty or parental unemployment.
- Being betrayed in relationships or robbed of goods and things that were precious to you.
- Suffering from poverty as an adult or experiencing unemployment, accidents, traumas, relationship breakdown, divorce or bereavement.

This is not an exhaustive list. There are many such possible events in a person's life. I am sure you could add to this list out of your own experience. Experiences like those above have the potential to scar our spirits and souls. A lot depends on how old we were when these things happened to us and the surrounding circumstances of our lives at the time. These and other factors will affect how much damage we received and how much that damage still influences us today.

The great news is that none of these things need to remain curses on our lives. Even if many years have passed, Jesus can still set the captives free.

There Is a Way Out

I have observed that the effect of trauma and painful events can vary enormously from one person to the next. If a person is already insecure and fearful when something awful happens, it is likely to have a much deeper and longer-lasting consequence in their lives. If someone is surrounded by loving care and comfort at a time when bad things happen, then they are more protected from deeper damage and will not need such deep healing later in life. But often that does not happen, and the pain can be buried very deeply in a person's innermost being.

In future segments of JOURNEY TO FREEDOM we will be looking more specifically at many of these things, including the consequences of ungodly parenting, abuse and traumas of varying types. For now, however, I want to encourage you by helping you see that as bad as these things can be, they are not impossible hurdles to overcome. Through my years of ministry, I have observed people being healed from every single one of these painful experiences.

Jesus is truly the Good Shepherd. He came in fulfillment of many prophetic words in the Old Testament. One such example is Ezekiel 34 where the prophet Ezekiel was given the tough assignment of prophesying against his own spiritual leaders.

The Lord's strongest words of condemnation came to Ezekiel because the shepherds of Israel had been caring for themselves and not for the people. They had used the tithes and the offerings to make themselves fat but had ignored the needs of the hurting and the broken. Ezekiel did not dress up his words in a form that was easy to take. This is what he said:

> "You have not strengthened the weak or healed the sick or bound up the injured. You have not brought back the strays or searched for the lost.

You have ruled them harshly and brutally. So they were scattered because there was no shepherd, and when they were scattered they became food for all the wild animals."

Ezekiel 34:4–5

In verses 15 and 16 of the same chapter, God showed the pain that He feels when His sheep are hurting and have not been healed.

Speaking through Ezekiel, He said, "I myself will tend my sheep and have them lie down, declares the Sovereign LORD. I will search for the lost and bring back the strays. I will bind up the injured and strengthen the weak."

This prophetic word about the Messiah was fulfilled when Jesus came and began to heal the hurting and to bind up the brokenhearted. He referred to Himself as the Good Shepherd and said, "I lay down my life for the sheep" (John 10:15).

For over thirty years now I have watched as Jesus, the Good Shepherd, has done exactly as He promised. He has come to the broken lambs. He has cared for the hurting and the abused, and He has led them gently in the safety of His loving care. He has set them free from the enemy, who is the thief who comes "to steal and kill and destroy" (John 10:10).

Susan had been given up for adoption by her natural parents who had had a sexual relationship in their teenage years. Eighteen years later, she was dying of a viral condition that was attacking her kidneys. As she forgave her parents for their sexual sin, she felt something happen inside her body. The power of any curse she had suffered under was broken by this simple act. She was healed instantly, and when she went to the hospital for her next appointment the doctors could no longer find any evidence of the viral condition that they had predicted would take her life within twelve months.

John retired early from a successful medical practice because he could no longer hold himself together. He had not been able to manage his depression, and it had led to suicidal thoughts. As we talked, he shared how his older brother had smashed his only toy as a child. His angry father beat him for crying. John had learned through this terrible experience not to share his emotions with anyone. But emotions are part of our God-given expression of life, and without them John was only half the man who God had intended. Depression had taken over his life. When he was able to forgive his brother and his father and to receive the love of Jesus into his heart, the tears that had been repressed over all of the years flowed. He was healed of his depression.

When people become Christians, their spirits that were formerly dead to God burst into new life. They become new creations. But even though everything becomes radically new, becoming a Christian does not change any of the details of their personal histories.

What God can and does do is to heal us of the consequences of the distress of the past. Satan wants to hang on to the control of those cords around our hearts that make us vulnerable to the powers of darkness. But the heart of Jesus is to see us healed and restored (see Isaiah 61:1–3). Little by little as you grasp hold of these wonderful truths and apply them in your life, you will see God change you from the inside out—forever.

SUMMARY

We have not escaped the things that have happened to us that have left scars on our lives. Satan wants to use all the bad and unhealed things from our pasts to hold us in bondage. Jesus died to set us free, and in Him there is real freedom (see John 8:36).

PRAYER

Help me, Lord, to identify those experiences that are still painful, unhealed memories. I want to bring each one of these to You for healing so that Satan will never be able to use them against me again. In Jesus' name, Amen.

WHAT HAVE I DONE? 25

No one likes the idea of swallowing one's pride and confessing sin, but unless we do, we are lost.

James 5:16 says, "Confess your sins to each other and pray for each other so that you may be healed." It would be easy to tell you that this is what the Bible says, so you should do it. But I recognize that it will take a closer look at the verse to break down its full meaning. It helps to have an understanding of what the words *sin* and *confession* mean. If we do not understand accurately what they mean, we could go through the motions of trying to tell God what we have done wrong without ever confessing the sin.

If you find that confusing, read on. It took me quite a long time to really understand the difference between giving God a list of things I have done wrong and actually confessing my sins. We will begin by asking ourselves some questions about truth.

What Is Truth?

Have you ever thought that there could be a difference between truth and falsehood and right and wrong? They sound as though they ought to mean essentially the same thing, but they do not. They can be very different according to your circumstances.

Pontius Pilate put to Jesus the most famous unanswered question ever asked: "What is truth?" (John 18:38). He did not realize that standing right in front of him was the man who was the very embodiment of truth. Jesus said, "I am the way and the truth and the life" (John 14:6). He also said, "I and the Father are one" (John 10:30). In Jesus and in God we have an absolute standard of knowledge, honesty and integrity. To use one short word, in Him we have truth. Truth is all three.

When a scientist is looking for the truth about a disease he is researching, the word *truth* means true knowledge. When a judge asks a witness in a court of law to tell the truth, the whole truth and nothing but the truth, she is asking the witness to be honest. When what people say and do is always consistent, and they do not change their story to suit themselves, they are acting with integrity. Integrity is truth unchanging. A person with integrity is the same all the way through. They have no outside covering that appears to be true to cover up a heart that is far from true.

When we apply these definitions of truth to God, we see that He knows all things and does not need to speculate about what might be the facts of a situation. What He says is always true. In Revelation 19:11, Jesus is called "Faithful and True."

God fears no one, so He is never tempted to deceive anyone else by telling a lie. God is consistent with Himself. He is the same all of the way through, which means that He has integrity.

He is the ultimate source of all knowledge and all understanding. Nothing is hidden from His eyes. You could say that truth is His name. There cannot be any variation in truth. Truth is absolute.

What about Right and Wrong?

While truth is absolute, right and wrong are relative. They are related directly to where you happen to be and whose authority you are under. If I am in England, it is fine to drive on the left-hand side of the road. It would be wrong to do that in France or in America where everyone drives on the right-hand side of the road. But there is nothing in Scripture to say that one is truth and the other is error, other than the biblical instruction that we are to obey governments that have authority.

I heard recently about a British woman in a Middle Eastern country who is serving a jail sentence for committing adultery. While committing adultery is contrary to God's covenant for the whole of the human race, it is not against the law in England. What is wrong in one country may be okay in another country. It all depends on the laws of the land.

In the United States of America, it can be legal to do some things in one state that are illegal in another state. Even within one country there can be variations in what is considered right and what is considered wrong.

A country is defined by the boundaries of an area over which a government has authority. Within that area of authority, the laws of the land determine what is right and what is wrong. It is up to an individual to know what the laws are. It is no defense for drivers to say they were driving within the speed limit of their own country if they were caught driving at an excess speed on a road in another country. Ultimately, what is right and what is wrong legally is determined by the laws of the authority you are under.

What about Sin?

Let us take a fresh look at Jesus. Already in *Building on the Rock*, we have demonstrated clearly that disciples of Jesus are not only those who trust in Him to be their Savior, but who have also invited Him to be Lord of their lives. They have chosen to come under His authority.

When Isaiah prophesied about the coming of the Messiah, this is what he said:

> For to us a child is born, to us a son is given, and the government will be on his shoulders. And he will be called Wonderful Counselor, Mighty God, Everlasting Father, Prince of Peace. Of the greatness of his government and peace there will be no end. He will reign on David's throne and over his kingdom, establishing and upholding it with justice and righteousness from that time on and forever.
>
> Isaiah 9:6–7

What Have I Done?

Isaiah saw in a vision that Jesus would not only be Savior, but that He would also be the head of an eternal government with authority over a territory that had no boundaries and no time limits. Jesus stated this Himself when He said that all authority had been given unto Him (see Matthew 28:18).

For a believer, right and wrong is not determined by our whereabouts on planet earth, because the Kingdom of God has no boundaries. It is determined by living in accordance with the truth. If we choose to live in a way that is contrary to the truth, as illustrated and defined by the life of Him who is truth, that action is defined as sin.

Sin, therefore, is defined as breaking the laws of God. Conversely, breaking the laws of the land may or may not be sin. It was certainly not sin when Daniel chose to break the law of the land that was put in place by Darius the king. The law stated that "anyone who prays to any god or human being during the next thirty days, except to you, Your Majesty, shall be thrown into the lions' den" (Daniel 6:7).

This law, however, did not cause Daniel to change the habits he had supported during his lifetime. "Three times a day he got down on his knees and prayed, giving thanks to his God, just as he had done before" (Daniel 6:10). The consequence of Daniel's action was the extraordinary night he had to spend in the den of lions when the angels shut the mouths of the lions and preserved his life.

From this we can see more clearly that sin is not defined by the king or the laws of any earthly country. There is a higher authority that matters even more than what is right or wrong according to the laws of any land. Sin is defined as all behavior—in thought, word or deed—that is in rebellion to the truth. That truth, as Isaiah described it, is the government of God.

There are absolutes in the world of science that are unchangeable facts. There are also statistics about the universe that are absolutes, such as the lowest possible temperature known as absolute zero. In the same way, there are absolutes in the spiritual realm. When Jesus referred to Himself as being the truth, He was stating one of those unchangeable absolutes by which all of humanity will be measured and judged.

We are all sinners who have fallen short of the mark. This term is the literal meaning of the word *sin* in Greek (see Romans 3:23). It must be obvious that not one of us could ever stand before a holy and righteous God at the end of time and claim that we were worthy of entering heaven's glory. We could not justify ourselves before the great Judge on the grounds of our behavior or life's work.

People may protest and plead that they are worthy because of their innocence, their good works, their kindness, their generosity or their attempts to bring peace into the world; however, every action or deed that has ignored the reality of Him who is truth will be seen for what it is—a tawdry imitation of righteousness. The pride of man, even in the realm of good works and religion, will try to achieve its own holiness in the sight of God. This is impossible for sinful man (see Ephesians 2:8–9).

As I have been writing these words, I have seen afresh how wonderful and amazing our salvation is. All of us will have to face God on that final day as we await our eternal destinies. It will only be those who are clothed in the sinless righteousness of Christ who will pass the test and be able to enter heaven.

Regardless of how fine we may claim the clothing of our own achievements to be, if we are clothed in our own righteousness, our achievements will be seen simply as filthy rags (see Isaiah 64:6; Philippians 3:9). There is no comparison to the transcendent glory of the Son of God.

Another way of looking at sin is nothing that is done outside of Christ will enter into heaven's glory. Or, as the old children's hymn by Mary Anne S. Deck expressed it:

> There is a city bright;
> Closed are its gates to sin;
> Naught that defileth,
> Naught that defileth,
> Can ever enter in.*

How precious it is to be in Christ. No wonder Paul rejoiced at the fact that his life was hidden with Christ in God (see Colossians 3:3).

*Mary Anne S. Deck, "There Is a City Bright," Hymnary.org, https://hymnary.org/text/there_is_a_city_bright_closed_are_its_ga.

Our Messiah is the only clothing we can wear that will stand the test of the judgment of our hearts in eternity.

The government of the whole universe does rest upon His shoulders, and those who believe in Him will be clothed in His righteousness.

What Does It Mean to Confess Sin?

The word *confess* in its original context means "to agree with." To confess sin to God is not coming simply to tell Him all of the things you have been doing that are wrong, as people might do who go to confession. God is all-knowing. He is not sitting on His throne waiting to find out from you what you have been doing. He knows that already.

Yes, we do need to own up to those things that are wrong. But what God is waiting for is for us to come before Him in humility agreeing fully with what He says about sin. We are to acknowledge our own sins, recognize that we miss the mark constantly and ask Him for forgiveness. Forgiveness means God releases us from the separation from Him that was caused by our sin. After we receive His forgiveness, God continues His relationship with us as if we had not sinned.

Imagine that you stole a huge sum of money from a bank. Afterward you came to the bank manager, admitted what you had done and asked him to take money out of his own pocket to pay back what you stole. After he paid your debt, you then asked him to continue in relationship with you as if you had never stolen the money in the first place. Against all logic, he agreed. That is what God does when He forgives us.

What a merciful God we have. It is hard to understand why He does not wipe us all off the surface of the planet, until we recognize that it is His love that is the reason. His love covers a multitude of our sins. He longs for that restoration of relationship with His children even more than we long for it.

When some people confess their sins, they do so understanding what the Bible defines as sin, such as breaking the Ten Commandments. They confess those sins to God, but in their heart of hearts they do not really agree that such things are wrong. Their confession is simply a list of things that God says is wrong. They do not have a heart that owns the true nature of either sin or their own personal sins.

Earlier in the book, we saw that everything we do in life, whether or not we are conscious of it, is an expression of worship. When we do things that are in accordance with the truth, we are worshiping God and will benefit from the blessing of His Spirit. But when we do those things that are contrary to the laws of God and are against the truth, we are worshiping the god of this world.

Instead of receiving blessings from God, we are in danger of receiving curses from the enemy. Satan always takes advantage of sin in order to create more pain for God's children. Our sin gives Satan his opportunity.

When people persist in sin, they break relationship with God. In addition, their disobedience does two other things:

- Takes us outside the protection of God (see Psalm 91:1)
- Puts us in a place of vulnerability to the enemy's attack (see Ephesians 4:27)

We not only need to ask God for forgiveness sin, but we also need to ask Him to cleanse us from the secondary consequences of sin. This is the message of 1 John 1:9. This verse refers to the need for both forgiveness and cleansing.

When we confess that we have sinned, we need to be specific about our sins. We need to ask God to set us free from every right that we have given to the enemy as a result of these sins. This is the process of healing that James talks about in James 5:14–16.

He urges those who are sick to call the elders to come to them so that they can confess all their known sins, ask for anointing with oil and then pray the prayer of faith for healing the sickness. All of these things can be part of the healing process.

The act of confessing our sins to one another deals with our pride. Pride is the biggest obstacle to the healing flow of God's Spirit. It was pride that was Satan's primary sin when he was thrown out of heaven, and mankind has taken on his characteristics. Jesus said to the Pharisees that their proud and boastful behavior came from their father, the devil (see John 8:44).

What Must I Do?

I believe that confession from the heart should be part of our daily routine of personal discipline before God. We should keep our confession up to date and keep short accounts with God. We should confess sin quickly before it has any opportunity to take root, or before it creates an opportunity for the enemy to cause sickness or invites a spirit of infirmity into our bodies.

Genesis 4:7 refers to the consequences of being in rebellion against God as sin crouching at the door. This is what Isaiah was talking about when he saw Jesus dying and said prophetically by faith, "by His wounds we are healed" (Isaiah 53:5).

To do this:

- We first need to come humbly before God and acknowledge that He is truth and that His understanding of sin is the one we want to agree with.
- We need to ask the Holy Spirit to shine His light into our lives and expose all darkness, all hidden motives and all obvious sin (Psalm 139:23–24).
- We need to own those things as being our responsibility and to admit that we are without excuse. We need to ask God for forgiveness and cleansing as David did in Psalm 51.
- We need to receive God's forgiveness in our hearts and, with God's help, to forgive ourselves. If we continue to hold ourselves in unforgiveness, we are saying Jesus' death on the cross was not sufficient for us. We put ourselves in the place of being judge over our own lives when we do this.
- If we are suffering from a physical illness from which we do not appear to be recovering naturally, then we need to follow the

scriptural injunction of James and call the elders to come. We need to share with them our confession and be anointed with oil for healing.

In all of my years of ministry, I have seen that there are two primary spiritual issues that people need to face as part of their preparation for receiving God's healing.

First: They need to forgive unconditionally all of those who have hurt them.
Second: They need to confess and receive forgiveness for those things in their lives that are an offense to the truth as seen in the life of Jesus and in the Word of God.

When people have been faithful and honest in these things, I have seen God bring major healing into their lives.

I will never forget being pressed by the Holy Spirit to teach without compromise what the Word of God says about sexual sin. It was a hard message to bring to a well-taught congregation. I am sure they already knew what the Scripture said, but perhaps they had not heard the truth and its consequences spelled out as clearly before.

At the end of that session, I invited all those who still had unconfessed sexual sin in their lives to come forward for prayer. There was a long silence, and then one man came to the front sobbing into his hands. At that point it was as if a dam broke. By the time the meeting was over, the majority of the congregation had come to the front to receive prayer.

What was most amazing about that time was not only the number of people who needed to confess sexual sins, but also the number of them who then went on to ask for prayer for physical healing. What followed was a great amount of healing and deliverance. Jesus, the Healer, was moving among His sheep. Confession, repentance and healing were all taking place as God's people got themselves cleaned up in the flow of His love and forgiveness. I have never forgotten the lesson of that day.

Looking Ahead

Later in JOURNEY TO FREEDOM, we will be looking at the whole area of sexuality and how the enemy can use ungodliness in this area to limit our potential in God. We are on a pilgrimage together, and I pray that as you think carefully through all we have shared together you will see it as a preparation for all that is to come.

SUMMARY

Confession of sin is much more than telling God what we have done wrong. It is coming to the place of agreement with God about what He thinks about our sin. When we have reached that understanding, it is a simple step forward to allow God to expose all darkness in our life so that He may forgive and cleanse us forever.

PRAYER

Help me, Lord, to see more clearly how unconfessed and unforgiven sin stands in the way of my relationship with You. I do not want anything in my past to be a barrier to going forward with You in my Christian walk. I pray that You will open my eyes to truly see myself as You see me. Give me the courage to live in the reality of that revelation by facing the need for confession of sin in my heart. Set me free to serve You in the liberty that flows from the cross. In Jesus' name, Amen.

STAGE 6

EQUIPPED TO SERVE

The first and last lesson in leadership is learning how to serve others.

COMMITTED
TO PEACE

HEALING FOR DISCIPLES

We are now moving forward in our understanding of what it means for believers to live as disciples of Jesus Christ. In some of the upcoming sections, you will recognize topics that we have already covered. The Jewish way of teaching was to tell the same truth several times in different ways so that people would see it from different perspectives. Considering that Jesus, who was a rabbi, undoubtedly did this, we will follow in His footsteps and revisit some truths that we learned earlier to help them gradually become part of who we are. It is like seeing the many different facets of a diamond from different angles.

This is what Jesus was doing in the book of Matthew when He told different parables that taught about the Kingdom of God. He was helping us gain a well-rounded understanding.

If you recognize some topics that have already been covered, please do not rush on, thinking that you already know all about that subject matter. Each time we look at a topic, we will either be seeing it from a different angle or going deeper into our understanding of it.

By Blue Galilee

I am writing this section in Israel, where all of the Jewish believers in Jesus refer to Him by His Hebrew name, Yeshua. It is wonderful to be able to share with many believers here the amazing truths of the Gospel in the land where Yeshua Himself walked and taught.

To sense the presence of God and to know His blessing as we worship Him with Arab, Jewish and Gentile believers is an amazing fulfillment of what the psalmist said in Psalm 133:1–3: "When God's people live together in unity . . . it is as if the dew of Hermon were falling on Mount Zion. For there the LORD bestows his blessing, even life forevermore." I love the older versions of the Bible that translate these words as God "commands blessing" because it gives Him so much joy.

The First Disciples

It is always such a thrill to be able to walk along the shores of Galilee where Jesus "saw Simon and his brother Andrew casting a net into the lake, for they were fishermen. 'Come, follow me,' Jesus said, 'and I will send you out to fish for people'" (Mark 1:16–17).

With their response to these simple words, a group of young men left behind their work as fishermen and became disciples of Jesus. They took up their new profession as fishers of men. They were ordinary people who responded to the call of Jesus. From that point on, they were known as His disciples. It was much later that they became known as apostles.

Not all disciples of Jesus become apostles, but you cannot be an apostle without first becoming a disciple. An apostle is someone with a special anointing for leadership and for bringing things into being that God has birthed in his or her heart. Apostles cannot be man-made or man-appointed, but when God's anointing is on them, their work can be recognized by others as being apostolic. Apostles have a special responsibility for pioneering leadership within the Body of Christ.

People should become disciples the moment that they respond to the call of Jesus. Sometimes, however, when people respond to the Gospel call for salvation they only think in terms of going to heaven when they die. Being a Christian disciple is much more than that—it is choosing to live with and for the Lord Jesus while on earth.

Choosing to respond to the call to follow and serve Jesus does not mean that you get an instant download of all of the knowledge and understanding that you will need as a disciple. Learning takes time and commitment. Jesus spent three years teaching and training His disciples for the task ahead. For those first disciples, it also meant a new career.

Training in Love

In many ways, JOURNEY TO FREEDOM is a course in discipleship. It is learning what we all need to know and understand about walking in the footsteps of Jesus. Yes, it takes time and commitment. Is it not, however, the least we can do in response to His incredible commitment to us? He chose to serve mankind by offering His sinless life so that sinners may come to know Him and have eternal life for themselves.

We often talk affectionately about the twelve disciples, but sometimes we forget that being a disciple must also mean coming under authority and discipline. Without discipline we will never fulfill the destiny God has for us.

In Hebrews 12 the writer is trying to help followers of Jesus see the way forward as disciples. He begins by telling them that they must get rid of everything that acts as a brake on their progress. He uses the illustration of a runner who could not win a race until he got rid of every obstacle that he was carrying.

Here are his words: "Let us throw off everything that hinders and the sin that so easily entangles. And let us run with perseverance the race marked out for us" (Hebrews 12:1). Training to be a disciple requires determination and a sense of purpose.

Later in the chapter, the writer tells us how important discipline is. He points out that a loving father disciplines his children. He then says that if we understand this principle for our own children, how much more gladly we should submit to the discipline of our loving heavenly Father. He says, "God disciplines us for our good, in order that we may share in his holiness" (Hebrews 12:10).

What an incredible reward awaits those who gladly seek to rid themselves of everything that stands in the way of their relationship with Father God. Such discipline "produces a harvest of righteousness and peace for those who have been trained by it" (Hebrews 12:11).

When God first gave me the vision for Journey to Freedom, I realized that it was for much more than a training program in healing. It was to build up the Body of Christ through equipping the saints in how to produce a harvest of righteousness. What an amazing and exciting objective.

Equipped to Serve

If disciples are being trained to follow in the footsteps of Jesus, what does this mean in real terms? Surely it must mean that we will want to follow His example. In his wonderful teaching in the letter to the Philippians, Paul gives an account of what coming to earth meant for Jesus:

> Who, being in very nature God, did not consider equality with God something to be used to his own advantage; rather, he made himself nothing by taking the very nature of a servant, being made in human likeness. And being found in appearance as a man, he humbled himself by becoming obedient to death—even death on a cross!
>
> Philippians 2:6–8

This amazing hymn of praise to Jesus ends with this declaration:

> Therefore God exalted him to the highest place and gave him the name that is above every name, that at the name of Jesus every knee should bow, in heaven and on earth and under the earth, and every tongue acknowledge that Jesus Christ is Lord, to the glory of God the Father.
>
> Philippians 2:9–11

Jesus came to serve others. The word *minister* means "servant." If someone becomes a minister of a local congregation, it means that he has been called to serve the people. He is to love, encourage, teach, heal and be their shepherd.

The highest point of Jesus' service to others was when He laid down His life so that we may rediscover ours. Having served the whole world in this extraordinary way, Jesus was raised up by God to His place in glory. Jesus did not raise Himself up from the dead—Father God did it (see Acts 2:24, 10:40; 1 Peter 1:21). In this we have an important principle. It is our responsibility to serve God in whatever way He leads us and whatever the cost. It is God's responsibility to raise us up and reward us (see James 4:10).

It is only through serving Him out of love that we put ourselves in the place of being blessed by the God who is love. Not all of the rewards may come in this life, but be assured that the rewards will come. Paul tells us in 1 Corinthians 3:14 that what we offer to God as the fruit of our lives will be tested, and each one will receive his or her reward.

First Samuel 2:30 says, "The LORD declares: . . . 'Those who honor me I will honor.'" This is not a vague promise that might happen. It is a commitment by God to give blessings to those who honor Him. It is also a declaration of the Lord's faithfulness to the promises He has made.

The Commission of a Disciple

When Jesus first sent out His disciples (see Luke 9:1–2), He gave them instructions to do three things: proclaim the Kingdom of God, heal the sick and cast out demons.

We have already looked at the importance of recognizing that as disciples of Jesus we are now citizens of a kingdom—not any of the kingdoms of this world, but of a spiritual kingdom whose authority exceeds that of Satan, the god of this world. We are like a colony of heaven living within the confines of an alien land.

God rejoices to bless His Kingdom citizens. He wants to equip them for life and to release them into their giftings and destinies. When you enter into that Kingdom, however, you come with the consequences of all the burdens of life. Some of the burdens are of your own making, some are caused by others and some are inherited. In order to fulfill your calling, you need to know the healing and personal restoration that Jesus, the Good Shepherd, wants His sheep to receive.

It is interesting that among the many prophetic words given to Ezekiel by the Sovereign Lord, some of the harshest and strongest words were reserved for the leaders of God's people in Israel. They were the ones who had responsibility for and authority over the sheep (the people) but who used their position irresponsibly to only take care of themselves (see Ezekiel 34:2).

God asks, through Ezekiel, "Should not shepherds take care of the flock?" (Ezekiel 34:2). They were happy to personally benefit from the offerings the people brought but were condemned by God because they had "not strengthened the weak or healed the sick or bound up the injured or brought back the strays or searched for the lost" (Ezekiel 34:4). The healing of His people was very much on the heart of God, and He has not changed His character or His nature. Healing is still on His heart today.

Later in Ezekiel 34 there is a clear Messianic prophecy about the coming of Jesus. Ezekiel speaks out words from the heart of God when he says that God will search for His sheep, pasture them, tend to them, search for the lost, bring back the strays, bind up the injured and strengthen the weak (see verses 11–16).

In these passages God is talking about the healing He wants His people to have when they return to their land (see Ezekiel 36:24). This is something that has been happening in our lifetimes. God not only wanted to see them return to their own land, but He also prophesied that when they returned to Him they would experience healing.

When Jesus came to the Jewish people in Israel, He referred to Himself as the Good Shepherd, the one who laid down His life for the sheep (see John 10:11). But then He said, "I have other sheep that are not of this sheep pen [meaning of Israel]. I must bring them also. They too will listen to my voice, and there shall be one flock and one shepherd" (John 10:16).

Jesus is painting an incredible picture of Jews and Gentiles who believe in the Messiah becoming one flock under the leadership of one

Shepherd. This is something that Paul explained in his letter to the Ephesians. He said that the ultimate purpose of God was

> to create in himself one new humanity out of the two [Jew and Gentile], thus making peace, and in one body to reconcile both of them to God through the cross . . . For through him we both have access to the Father by one Spirit.
>
> Ephesians 2:15–18

Later in JOURNEY TO FREEDOM, we will take a closer look at God's purposes for Israel. For now, however, it is important to see that healing is clearly on the heart of God for all of His people—Jew and Gentile. When we come back to Him, we come with all of the consequences of having lived in an alien land. We come without a reliable moral compass, and we come from a place where the god of this world has tried constantly to put us into chains of bondage. Jesus said that He had come to set us free from these chains (see Luke 4:18; John 10:10).

Getting Ready for Service

His healing is for us all—for you and for me. It is on the heart of God for all believers without exception. It is for the shepherds and the sheep, for both the Jew and the Gentile. If we really want to enter into the place of peace with God through Jesus, the Good Shepherd, then it is essential that we give Him His rightful place in our lives as Lord, Savior and Healer.

SUMMARY

God has a purpose for your life. You need training for the task—training that Jesus gave to the first disciples on the job. But in addition to the training, you need to be personally transformed. This means that you must be willing to walk the walk of discipleship and receive the healing you need. Only in this way can you truly serve Him as a disciple.

PRAYER

Thank You, Lord, that You call ordinary men and women to serve You as disciples. Help me to see my life as an opportunity for You to bring healing to others as I seek to serve You as a disciple. In Jesus' name, Amen.

HEALING FOR THE INNER MAN

Jeff was the apple of his parents' eyes. They loved God and they loved their son. It seemed that everyone loved him. He enjoyed life and was fun to be with.

In his teens he fell in with friends who seemed like cool characters, but they took advantage of his generous heart and led him into some very ungodly things. By his twenties Jeff had become a man of the world. He was no longer a sweet-faced boy, but was now very worldly-wise and had forgotten God. He was more experienced with women than he should have been, and some of the words that came out of his mouth would have embarrassed his mother and father. By his thirties he had made a small fortune through some very dubious business deals. He had been married and divorced already, because the mother of his children could not handle his unfaithfulness. By his forties he had lost both his fortune and his family and could only sustain short-term jobs between bouts of drinking.

In his fifties he came to himself. His mom and dad were dead, so he searched for his long-forgotten sister. As he stood on her doorstep, she hardly recognized him. The sweet-faced kid she had known so well was gone, and in his place were the scars of a hard and selfish life lived without God.

She wept. He wept. And thus began his journey from the island of pain to the harbor of peace. Several weeks later he knelt with his sister and gave his life back to the Lord he had known as a child. She had led the prodigal home to the Savior. He came as he was to the foot of the cross. He began the journey of recovery to put his life back together.

He could not undo history or change anything from his past, but little by little the Savior healed his broken heart and put him back on the road of life. The years that the locusts had eaten had taken their toll, but the love of his Savior brought healing to the damage his heart had sustained. He spent the latter years of his life warning young people of the dangers of false friends and of ignoring God's call on their lives. His heart was now anchored firmly in God, and he saved many from the traps of the enemy.

This story of Jeff is only fiction, but every component of the story is based on personal ministry experience and is true for someone—maybe even for you.

In the past thirty years of my life, I have spoken with hundreds, probably thousands, of people who were in deep need of personal healing. One of the most common things that people say is, "Why didn't someone teach me about these things when I was young?"

If a person's heart is not anchored securely in God, then it is too easy to drift across the sea of life until his or her vessel is shipwrecked on the rocks of joyless pleasure. Even when that happens, it is not the end of the road for the believer in God. He still wants to equip us to serve Him in the best possible way for however many more years we have left on the earth.

The Heart of Man

It is hard to define precisely what the heart of man is, but most everyone knows what it means to make a decision of the heart. When you talk about someone's heart, you are talking about the very core of their personality—that inner place of their being where their emotions have a great influence. It is the place where we think our most private thoughts, where our secret inner motives are rooted and where our decisions are made.

It is the meeting place of our spirits and our souls. It is the place where our minds, our emotions and our wills converge to determine the issues of life. Above all, it is the place where we choose to be responsive to either the sweet influence of the Spirit of God or to the dangerous influence of the god of this world, who then uses the motives of our hearts to further lead our fallen, carnal natures astray.

The Bible has a lot to say about the heart—the inner man. The writer of the Proverbs warns us "Above all else, guard your heart, for everything you do flows from it" (Proverbs 4:23). He then warns men of the dangers of an adulteress by saying, "Do not let your heart turn to her ways or stray into her paths. Many are the victims she has brought down . . . Her house is a highway to the grave" (Proverbs 7:25–27). He is warning about the serious and dangerous secondary consequences of following the ungodly desires of the heart.

Jeremiah described the heart of man as being "deceitful above all things and beyond cure" (Jeremiah 17:9). In verse 10 the Lord says, "I the LORD search the heart and examine the mind, to reward each person according to their conduct, according to what their deeds deserve." This means that the choices of the heart are within our control. If it did not mean that, the idea of receiving a reward according to our conduct would make no sense.

But if God says that the heart of man is beyond cure, then what are we praying for when we ask for inner healing? Are we trying to heal something that cannot be healed?

Even the apostle Paul recognized that there is a problem in this respect. He admitted his own difficulty in dealing with the motives that were resident in his own sinful nature. "For I have the desire to do what is good, but I cannot carry it out. For I do not do the good I want to do, but the evil I do not want to do—this I keep on doing" (Romans 7:18–19).

In verses 22–24 he said:

> For in my inner being I delight in God's law; but I see another law at work in me, waging war against the law of my mind and making me a

prisoner of the law of sin at work within me. What a wretched man I am! Who will rescue me from this body that is subject to death?

Mercifully, his response to this question is clear and positive. "Thanks be to God, who delivers me through Jesus Christ our Lord!" (Romans 7:25). There was an answer to Paul's problem, and there is a solution for us all. The answer is not a clever argument, but rather a person—the only person who has ever overcome sin and death. It is only through Jesus that we can enjoy the blessing of living under a higher law. Paul said the Spirit has "set you free from the law of sin and death" (Romans 8:2).

Let us summarize what all this means for you and for me.

Because of the Fall, our hearts have acquired a nature that has been corrupted by man's allegiance to the god of this world. We call it the *sin nature* or the *carnal nature*. The spirit within our human nature as created originally by God still craves after Him. But the corruption in our hearts that came through the Fall means that there is a conflicting law also operating in our hearts. Our carnal natures desire to please our father, the devil, which is how Jesus described Satan when He was telling the Pharisees exactly where their ungodly thinking had its origins (see John 8:42–47).

The constant battle in the heart of every human being, whether or not they are a born-again believer, is between the desire to do things that would please the God who loves and made them, and the desire to please the one who wanted to be above the Almighty and take the worship that was due to God. In simple terms, the consequence is that our carnal nature desires to worship Satan and is intent on influencing us to do things that would please Satan.

When we are convicted of sin by the Holy Spirit and repent and receive Jesus as our Lord and Savior, we are born again of the Spirit of God. Our human spirits, which had been made dead to God through sin, have new and living relationships with Father God. We are then in the position of not having to live according to the demands of "the flesh but according to the Spirit" (Romans 8:4).

We can, of course, still make ungodly choices and sin when we allow the carnal nature to have its way. Through the power of the Spirit, however, we can resist the devil and choose to make the right decisions. Because Jesus never came under Satan's control, His authority is always higher than Satan's.

As long as we are living on planet earth we are living in the territory controlled by Satan, the god of this world. We will always have a carnal nature. It is only when we, the redeemed, leave this life and enter paradise that we will lose the carnality of our natures. Nothing in heaven will be tainted by the sins of mankind. We will be totally free from all of the consequences of sin. There will be no need for the healing ministry in heaven, for no one will be suffering. It will truly be paradise for all believers.

Who and What Can Be Healed?

If the carnal nature cannot be cured in this life, then what can be healed? The answer is simple—whatever damage we have experienced that has either been as a result of our own wrong choices or the ways the sins of others have affected us. These are our wounds.

There are sins and there are wounds. Scripture tells us that "those who belong to Christ Jesus have crucified the flesh with its passions and desires" (Galatians 5:24). That means that we are to put sinful choices to death. To be put in even simpler terms, we are to say no to the flesh and the enemy.

While we can put sin to death, we cannot put our wounds to death. The wounds are there as a result of our history. No amount of trying to crucify the pain that we now have as a result of those wounds will ever work. Trying to do so is like trying to stop dandelion growth in a lawn by pulling the flower heads off the plants. All that does is strengthen the roots and make the problem worse. To deal with the dandelions, you have to extract the roots. To deal with the pain of the past, the root must be exposed so that the wound can be healed.

You cannot change or cure the fact that we have a carnal nature, but God can heal the damage that the carnal nature's wrong choices have caused. Under the Lordship of Jesus, we can cease to give way to the inner demands that the carnal nature tries to make on our lives.

This is the process that the early church fathers referred to as *sanctification*. Paul described it as "being transformed into his image with ever-increasing glory, which comes from the Lord, who is the Spirit" (2 Corinthians 3:18).

Jesus' death on the cross dealt with all of the consequences of sin. In Him our relationships with Father God can be restored, and through Him our wounds can be healed. This is exactly what the prophet Isaiah was talking about in Isaiah 53:5 when he said about the Messiah, "He was pierced for our transgressions . . . and by his wounds we are healed."

God does not want us to continue suffering because of the wounds we have sustained in the battle of life. Jesus sent this very clear message into our fallen world by beginning His ministry healing the sick. This expression of the heart of God for His children is a clear message to mankind of the love of our heavenly Father. No wonder He was upset with the leaders of Israel for not bringing God's healing to the hurting (see Ezekiel 34). They were not representing the true heart of God to the hearts of men.

Many years ago, the work of Ellel Ministries was described as bringing the heart of God to the heart of man. That phrase has become our most enduring slogan, and it describes the nature of God's ministry to a hurting world.

In summary, the nature of the heart of man cannot be changed, but all of the consequential damage can be healed. In Christ we can have the strength to resist the pressure to sin that comes from our carnal nature. Who is this blessing for? For all who come to Him for salvation and healing—for all of those who choose to walk in His ways.

Back to Jeff

In the opening story, we saw how a man made wrong choices when he was faced with temptation. He allowed his carnal nature to lead him astray. When Jeff returned to the Lord, forgiveness was instant and unconditional; however, all of the damage Jeff had sustained throughout his life was not healed instantly.

Inner healing is a process. The issues have to be faced and dealt with. People need to be forgiven. Sins need to be confessed. The ties to people with whom ungodly relationships were forged need to be broken. Healing and possibly deliverance will need to be applied to the wounds.

Jeff's wounds will be healed little by little, and he will begin to rediscover who God intended him to be. He will begin to enter into his destiny. And while Jeff's face may still bear the scars of life, the sparkle in his eyes will reflect that he knows the joy of the Lord that will be his strength.

He will need to continue to resist the temptations of the flesh in the power of the Spirit of God. If at any time he falls back into sin, he will need to come back to God quickly and get his life back on track again. I can assure you, however, that since God is his Helper, Healer and Deliverer, Jeff will rejoice again. I have seen it happen too many times not to believe it. With God all things are possible.

If God can do that for people like Jeff who have plumbed the depths of sin, then there can be no obstacle to healing the lesser things that also seek to be a barrier to our growth as disciples of Jesus.

SUMMARY

Inner healing as part of your daily walk with God is essential if you are going to grow to maturity as a man or a woman of God. You cannot change your past, but God is able and willing to heal you of the damage that the past has caused.

PRAYER

Thank You, Lord, that You love me so much that You do not want me to remain in bondage to my past. Help me to distinguish between my sins and my wounds so that, with Your help, I can truly crucify the ungodly choices that arise from my carnal nature and be healed of the damage I have suffered because of my past. In Jesus' name, Amen.

SET FREE TO SERVE

We have learned together how the carnal nature in the heart of man cannot be healed, but that the damage caused by what has happened to us in the past can be healed. It is obvious that unless we receive healing for these things, our potential will be limited, and our capacity to serve will be restricted.

At the beginning of Hebrews 12 we are urged to get rid of everything that gets in the way of our ability to run, especially the sin that entangles us (see Hebrews 12:1). Verses 12 and 13 of Hebrews sum this up well: "Strengthen your feeble arms and weak knees. 'Make level paths for your feet,' so that the lame may not be disabled, but rather healed."

It is clear from the context of this passage that the writer is referring primarily to spiritual lameness rather than actual physical conditions. I have, however, seen many examples of how dealing with issues in a person's life has enabled them to receive physical healing.

One couple longed to have a baby but were unable to conceive. The lady had been engaged previously but broke it off when she realized that he was not the man God wanted her to marry.

As they were ending their relationship, the man said to her, "If you will not marry me, then you will never be a mother." Those words had acted as a curse on her life. When she forgave the man, the power of his words was broken, and she was set free and healed. Very shortly after that she conceived her first child.

Healing the "Disabled"

When I am speaking at conferences and church meetings, I often use people from the audience to teach various points. In one of the simplest yet most effective dramas that I use, I ask a young man to help me. I instruct him to try to run across the stage. Before he does that, though, I also ask four other people onto the stage who are instructed to hold his legs and arms to prevent him from moving forward.

One of the people holding on to a limb might represent unconfessed wrong relationships from his past. Another person might represent an unforgiven wound. The third could represent his experiences dabbling in the occult. The last person might represent a dominating mother who still controls him.

With these four hindrances (the people) hanging on tightly to his legs and arms, I urge him to run. It is, of course, impossible for him to move forward. He remains anchored to the spot by his problems. No amount of extra Bible study, attending prayer meetings, fasting or anything else will help him run the race more effectively. What needs to happen is that the issues represented by those who are holding his arms and legs must be addressed, and the obstructions must be removed.

It is easy to see in the illustration what happens when the different issues are dealt with. The man is set free to run the race of life and to be equipped to serve in the Kingdom of God.

This picture, however, is not only an illustrative drama. It is the real situation for many, many people who are nursing known or unknown issues from their pasts. The Body of Christ is full of unhealed people who would love to be able to take a more active role in the Kingdom of God.

The whole purpose behind JOURNEY TO FREEDOM is to equip the saints of God to be warriors for God as disciples of Jesus Christ.

The Swine Flu Health Check

Shortly before I began writing, the governments of many countries started to react to the outbreak of a worldwide pandemic. It was a flu virus that started its life in Mexico and was called Swine Flu. I received a booklet through my mail box from the government that told me all that I needed to know about Swine Flu and what to do if I had any symptoms.

It was only when I arrived back from one of my teaching trips overseas and was not feeling well that I thought suddenly that I had better read what that leaflet said. Because I was now struggling with some flu-like symptoms, the leaflet had assumed an importance it did not have previously.

When I found it and read the details, the leaflet was not helpful. It told me nothing that would help me decide whether or not I had caught the virus. It did, however, give me an internet address and told me to go online to check my symptoms against a series of diagnostic questions that I could answer through my computer. Twenty minutes later it was clear to me that whatever it was that I had was not Swine Flu.

The online checklist did help me think through how best to summarize what we have been learning together. The next section contains the Journey to Freedom Seven Point Health Check.

The Journey to Freedom Seven Point Health Check

In putting this together, I imagined what questions the writer of Hebrews might have put on a checklist for his lame, feeble or weak readers. Or perhaps what Paul might have devised for the Galatian or the Ephesian Christians who were struggling with temptation and the consequences of sin.

All of the following are vital questions, starting with the first one that asks basic questions about whether or not we really know the Lord.

> QUESTION 1
>
> **Do I know the Lord for myself, or do I only know about Him?**

I will never forget the clergyman who came with his wife on a Healing Retreat at Ellel Grange. He had been a minister for 35 years. When he heard the retreat's first teaching, however, he realized that there was a major problem in his life. He knew all about Jesus but did not know Him personally.

Salvation is a gift that is received through faith in Jesus Christ, through whom we enter into a living relationship with God. Salvation is not something we can earn or buy (like getting an entrance ticket to heaven). Nor is it something we get as a reward for being religious or for putting in years of service in the church.

Throughout the worldwide work of Ellel Ministries, we have now conducted over 3,000 Healing Retreats. On almost every one, there have been individuals who came for healing but discovered that the primary healing they needed was to be born again of the Spirit of God. This is like a resurrection from the dead—there cannot be any greater healing need than resurrection.

While in Israel, we met a Russian-speaking lady who had attended one of our events in Ukraine fifteen years earlier. She had come to a healing conference and discovered that salvation was her primary healing need. She was born again. Today, many years later, she is a pastor's wife in Israel.

If you still have any doubts about whether or not you really know the Lord, may I encourage you to go back to stage two of our journey together and read those chapters again? If you do not know the Lord, then you cannot receive the healing He longs to give to His children.

QUESTION 2

I am trusting Jesus to be my Savior so that when I die I can be assured of a place in heaven. In the meantime, am I willing for Jesus to be Lord of every area of my life here on earth?

This is a big and enduring problem. Even though we are living within the limitations of time and space, God has put eternity in the hearts of every man and woman (see Ecclesiastes 3:11). The big question of what happens when we die is never far from the surface of our minds, especially when we are in potentially dangerous circumstances.

When evangelists present Jesus as the key to eternity and the Savior from death and hell, they are proclaiming truth—but it is not the whole truth. As a result, many people respond to an altar call or pray the Sinner's Prayer only as a means of avoiding hell. They hedge their bets just in case after death they find that hell is a real place. The important question to ask is not whether or not we are going to heaven or hell, but do we love Jesus?

Some of the most challenging words in Scripture come from the lips of Jesus when He says, "Not everyone who says to me, 'Lord, Lord,' will enter the kingdom of heaven, but only the one who does the will of my Father who is in heaven" (Matthew 7:21).

Jesus is stating a fact that is seldom taught. The evidence for our salvation is not shown by whether or not we have a decision card, but by whether or not we desire to do the will of the Father on earth. Jesus put it very simply when He said, "Anyone who loves me will obey my teaching. My Father will love them, and we will come to them and make our home with them. Anyone who does not love me will not obey my teaching" (John 14:23–24).

You cannot separate love and obedience in Scripture. It was Jesus' love for mankind that made Him obedient to death on the cross. It should be our love for Him that makes us want to be obedient and serve Him. If it is evident by the way we live that we have no interest in loving and obeying God while we are here on earth, then it is not unreasonable to ask for what reason should God open the doors of heaven to us when we die.

In terms of healing, the key question arising out of this is whether or not Jesus is Lord of our lives here and now. Do we love Him enough to want to obey Him? Will we allow Him to be the Lord of our lives and not just a Savior to whom we will turn suddenly when we die? If He is not Lord, then we do not have any authority over the works of darkness in our lives. We may pray for healing, but we will not be in the place to receive the healing for which we are asking.

QUESTION 3

Have I forgiven all of those down my generational line who have done ungodly things that have resulted in my receiving an ungodly inheritance?

It is true that the person you are can be influenced seriously by the way others have lived before you. One generation after another can be influenced by and suffer from the consequences of the sins of the ancestors (see Exodus 20:5; Lamentations 5:7).

If we know there are issues in our lives related directly to a negative inheritance given by our ancestors, we need to speak out our forgiveness. We then need to forgive everyone else who has done anything that might have released any ungodly spiritual influences into our ancestral lines.

I prayed for a sixteen-year-old named James who had been an epileptic since childhood. At the time that I prayed for him, he had finished an epileptic seizure and was unconscious. I led his spirit in a prayer to forgive everyone on his generational line who had done anything that had made him vulnerable to the condition. Even when a person is unconscious, you can still talk to their spirit, which never goes unconscious. Paul makes an interesting comment on the relationship between the spirit and the mind of man when he says, "For who knows a person's thoughts except their own spirit within them?" (1 Corinthians 2:11).

I then prayed for deliverance and healing. James was healed completely, a miracle that was confirmed by the doctors on his next visit to the hospital. His healing was so profound that the doctors wrote on his medical records that James could never have been an epileptic, even though when I prayed for him he was unconscious due to an epileptic fit. It was the act of forgiving his ancestors and then praying for deliverance and healing that released God's healing in James.

QUESTION 4

Have I forgiven my own parents, brothers and sisters for anything they did to me that has left me with lifetime scars?

People who hurt us the most are often the ones who are closest to us. Parents do not get everything right. One of the traps they can fall into is treating unfairly or looking unfavorably toward one of their children. This can happen if they were wanting a girl and they got a boy or vice-versa.

Some of the most difficult cases we have to deal with are when the parents who should be protecting their children turn out to be cruel and abusive, even sexually abusing their own offspring. Brothers and sisters can also be very cruel, especially when they become jealous or start punishing one of their siblings.

The closer the people are to us, the harder it sometimes is to forgive them. When Jesus instructed us to forgive all of those who have hurt us (see Matthew 6:15), He was showing us how we can be set free from the consequences of inner bitterness and unforgiveness.

QUESTION 5

Have I forgiven all who have hurt me—from elementary years through college, within the realms of work, family life and church life?

Outside of the family there can be many people who have caused us pain. If this is still an issue for you, I suggest you go back and read again the teaching based on the Lord's Prayer.

QUESTION 6

Have I been honest with myself and with God about all the known sins in my life? Have I confessed them before God and man so that they might be forgiven (see 1 John 1:9) and healed (see James 5:16)?

Am I willing for God to shine His light into every area of my life so that any other darkness that remains as a result of my sins can be exposed and dealt with? It is important we say yes to this question because we are often self-deceived. We need to give Jesus permission to show us what we need to know about ourselves (see Psalm 139:23–24).

We do not have a natural desire to face things we thought had been long-forgotten, but sometimes it is those long-forgotten things that the enemy can hang on to. He will want to use them to maximum effect to keep us bound to the past.

The prophet Isaiah became more aware of the sinfulness of his life when he had the extraordinary experience of being in the presence and holiness of God (see Isaiah 6:5). The closer we get to God, the more aware we become of areas of our lives that need to be cleansed. This is part of the whole process of sanctification, through which we are not only being made holy (growing more like God day by day) but also receiving our healing.

QUESTION 7
Am I willing to serve the Lord all of my days, seeking out His best for my life and choosing to serve Him joyfully?

It is easy to think that if we give God the best of our lives, we will be depriving ourselves of the pleasures of life. There is worldly logic within this conclusion, but it is not true. It is another deception of the enemy.

The greatest joy any of us can ever experience is through being fulfilled in God. He has given us gifts and abilities, and when we are using these to live in the destiny that He has prepared for us in advance (see Ephesians 2:10), we will know the greatest joy. When we are willing for Him to have His way in our lives, we will know the greatest depth of healing and joy any of us can ever experience.

Be Systematic

Answering the above questions may not be the solution to every situation you will face in life, but if you deal with all the issues raised by these seven questions, you will see life transformation. I have seen often how God brings important things to the surface of people's memories when they pray systematically through their lives. In this process they realize that they have unresolved issues from their past—things that deep down in their subconscious they may have stressed about or wrestled with for years.

In many cases the consequence of buried sin is unresolved pain or other physical conditions for which people may have sought medical treatment. It always amazes me how often physical symptoms disappear when we resolve the spiritual issues in our lives. We may describe this as having been healed, but in reality it is the removal of the hidden underlying issues that are reflected in the body as pain.

More to Come

There is much more we need to learn about the nature of man—but all in good time. We will see how the mind, emotions and will work together in the soul, and how the spirit, soul and body operate together, giving us our humanity.

We are taking these steps carefully—one at a time—so we can understand the scriptural principles involved and then apply them in our lives. This is both for our own benefit and for the sake of others to whom God may call us to help along life's journey. This is how the Body of Christ works—helping one another (see Ephesians 4:16).

Next we will be looking at how we must always be ready for action as we listen to the Lord and seek to serve Him with everything we have.

SUMMARY

In order to be equipped to serve God, we need to be set free from all of the obstacles that are standing in the way of both our healing and our commitment to the Lord. When we choose to obey Him because we love Him, we put ourselves in the place of blessing.

PRAYER

Thank You, Lord, that Your love for me does not depend on my having had a perfect past. Thank You for loving me as I am and for being willing to help me get to the place where I fulfill my destiny in You. In Jesus' name, Amen.

READY FOR ACTION

In recent chapters we have looked at some of the essential stepping stones toward personal transformation. It is vital that we understand how we can receive His healing for ourselves and be equipped to serve Him. We need to be ready at all times for whatever action the Lord calls us to take.

It is no use thinking that when God calls me, I will get ready, but until that happens I will live to entertain myself. The fact is that God calls those who have already shown by their heart attitudes that they are willing. He calls those who are preparing themselves as men and women of God for whatever He may call us to do. That does not mean we are not going to have any fun in life. As we will see tomorrow, the best things in life are always found by being in the place of God's calling.

As we seek to find the destiny that God has planned for us, we may not know what our life's work will turn out to be. All that God requires of us is to be obedient to Him one day at a time and to trust Him with the outcome. In my own journey, even though I knew God was calling me into a healing ministry, I could only take one step at a time, one day at a time.

Even today my life is like that. I marvel at His goodness when I look back and see the way He led me safely through the enemy's minefield to reach a field of blessing. That does not mean there have been no mistakes along the way. One of the most important lessons I learned was that even when I make a mistake, I am still loved by God. The sooner I recognize the mistake and get back on track through confession and repentance, the sooner I will be back in the place of my calling.

The Christian life is never boring. It is an amazing adventure with God. It is an adventure in which God gives us wonderful opportunities to participate in what He is doing. He delegated His authority over the earth to mankind, and it is through mankind that He does His work on earth. This is why He looks for our cooperation to get things done.

When it comes to taking action for the Kingdom, God looks for those who are equipped, ready and willing. He looks for those who are waiting patiently for that divine moment of opportunity so they can spring into action in obedience to their master.

None of us can spring into action unless our feet are active, fit and well-shod. I have a friend who struggles due to a problem with his feet, and because of this he is extremely limited in what he can do. It is the same if our spiritual feet are incapacitated in any way. We are limited in what we can do in the Kingdom of God. Our spiritual feet need to be in good shape and well-shod.

With Feet Shod

How can we have well-shod feet? In the final chapter of Ephesians, Paul tells us in detail how to defend ourselves against all the spiritual attacks of the enemy. As part of the armor available to a believer, he says to have "your feet fitted with the readiness that comes from the gospel of peace" (Ephesians 6:15).

I love the way the Amplified Bible translates Ephesians 6:15: "And having shod your feet in preparation [to face the enemy with the firm-footed stability, the promptness, and the readiness produced by the good news] of the Gospel of peace" (AMPC).

Then we read in Isaiah 52:7, "How beautiful on the mountains are the feet of those who bring good news, who proclaim peace, who bring good tidings, who proclaim salvation." In Nahum 1:15, we read, "Look, there on the mountains, the feet of one who brings good news, who proclaims peace!"

It is clear from these verses that the feet are very important. They must be well-shod at all times for the work of the Kingdom. There is a sense in which we must never take our shoes off.

If you are a member of the fire, ambulance or police emergency services, you cannot be on duty and not have your shoes on. You must always be ready to spring into action. It is no use saying, "Just wait a minute while I get my shoes on," when a person's life may be threatened by any delay.

The same principle applies to all of the weapons of warfare that Paul describes in Ephesians 6. We should remain armed spiritually at all times. We should remain relaxed in God, but ready at all times for a rapid response. The only difference between believers and the emergency service personnel is that believers never go off duty.

We may have seasons in our lives when we are more relaxed than at others, for we all need rest and recovery. We all would enjoy an annual vacation or a Sabbath rest. But if we think that our vacation, for example, is a time when we can go spiritually off duty, then beware. These can be the seasons of life when we are caught off guard by the enemy who is trying actively to get us into wrong activities or wrong relationships. Satan never takes a vacation. I am reminded of the wise and very true comment John Bunyan made in *Pilgrim's Progress* when he was talking about the dangers of being caught off guard and falling into sin: "One leak will sink a ship!"*

The lesson of the *Titanic* must never be forgotten. This seemingly unsinkable vessel was navigating in the darkness through a minefield of icebergs. It only took a collision with one iceberg to sink the vessel, causing massive loss of life. Instead of being associated with something unsinkable, the name *Titanic* has entered the world's vocabulary for the opposite reason. Being caught off guard turned a simple

---

*John Bunyan, *Pilgrim's Progress* (Mineola, N.Y.: Dover Publications, 2003), 314.

but catastrophic mistake into one of the world's greatest peacetime disasters.

Sadly, there have been many Titanics in the history of Christian ministry. The media loves to give huge publicity to these events, and great damage has been done to the Body of Christ because of them. No wonder the Scripture reminds us of the dangers of pride when it says, "So, if you think you are standing firm [on those feet of yours] be careful that you don't fall!" (1 Corinthians 10:12).

While there is confession, repentance, forgiveness and restoration available for the believer, there are also times when an unguarded moment can take a person off course for years, sometimes even a lifetime. Where our feet take us is always of critical importance to God. They can either take us to places of blessing or places of cursing.

The title of Derek Prince's very important book *Blessing or Curse: You Can Choose!* (Chosen, 2006) says it all as he describes the consequences of either remaining in or going outside of the provisions of God's covenant. We will be looking very carefully at how God wants to bless us through His covenant promises at a later stage.

We cannot walk anywhere without using our feet. Wherever our feet go, the rest of our body will follow. The feet cannot go one way and the body another. The feet are the agency of the body that take us wherever we choose to go.

It is especially significant that the book of Proverbs includes "feet that are quick to rush into evil" (Proverbs 6:18) among the seven things that are detestable to God. We need to put our feet down on safe ground and not let them take us into places of spiritual compromise or sinful activity.

The psalmist declared that "Your word is a lamp for my feet, a light on my path" (Psalm 119:105). We will do well to always heed the Word of God and let it be a constant light on our paths. For this to become reality in our lives, we need to regularly take in Scripture and let it become a bastion of truth in our hearts. If you have any questions about the importance of obeying God's Word, it may be helpful for you to read again some of the teaching in stage three, "The Bible—My Guide for Life."

The Gospel of Peace

Let us get back to those shoes we all need to be wearing. Paul tells us that our feet must be shod with the readiness that comes from the Gospel of peace. What does this mean?

We can only know the peace of God for ourselves, which truly does pass all understanding (see Philippians 4:7), through knowing God and seeking to bring our lives into line with His truth. We cannot know the inner peace that transcends all the issues of life without being in relationship with the God of peace.

If we are going to be an agency of peace for others, we must come to know this peace in our own lives. Otherwise our efforts to tell others about the peace of God will sound like a man who tells people about how safe the roller coaster is but is too scared to have a ride himself.

In the early days of his ministry, the great evangelist Billy Graham wrote one of those Christian books that will go down in history as a life-changing volume. *Peace with God: The Secret Happiness* became an instant bestseller and has continued to sell by the thousands. I do not think it has ever been out of print.

It was first published in 1953 before Billy Graham's momentous evangelistic campaign in 1954 at the Harringay Arena in London. The book explained how all human beings are in need of peace in their hearts, and the only way to obtain peace is by forgiveness of sin through Jesus Christ.

Nigel Johnson was a young Cambridge graduate who attended the meetings on one of the nights when I went with my dad. I was a ten-year-old boy at the time. I marvelled at the hundreds of men and women at those meetings who found faith in Jesus Christ and peace with God. The experience had a deep impact on me.

We did not know Nigel, but on the way into the meetings, Dad responded to a prompting from the Holy Spirit (he was ready for action) to follow him in and pray for him. We sat behind him and Dad prayed. Nigel did not respond to the Gospel message. After the meeting, Dad followed him out of the arena and sat next to him on the underground train (even though it was going the opposite direction from our own journey home). Dad asked him if he had enjoyed the meeting. Nigel did not respond.

Dad gave him his card and said, "We will be praying for you." With an undecipherable grunt, Nigel got off the train at the next stop. Dad continued to pray.

Two years later we received a tape-recorded testimony from Nigel Johnson telling how that simple question about whether or not he had enjoyed the meeting had prompted him to go back to Harringay the following night and listen once more to Billy Graham. That night, he told us, he gave his life to Christ and found peace with God.

The spiritual shoes Dad had been wearing that night were shoes of peace. He was willing to go out of his way—and the wrong direction on the train—simply because of the prompting of the Spirit to pray for Nigel. He kept praying until Nigel found peace with God. That is something that we should all be ready and willing to do—to share the good news of peace and salvation with whomever God puts across our paths. I have never forgotten that lesson. Paul tells us that to take ground from the enemy in this way is a key part of the armory of the disciple. We must always be ready.

Readiness at All Times

As a child playing with school friends, I recall that one of the phrases that we used to let everyone know the game was beginning was *action stations*. That meant we had to be ready. You never know when the master is going to speak out the equivalent of these words into your spirit to call you into action.

What I do know, however, is that if you are not ready when that call comes, you will miss an opportunity to be the feet, the hands or the voice of God in bringing His love into the heart of one of His children. Peter encouraged us to "Always be prepared to give an answer to everyone who asks you to give the reason for the hope that you have. But do this with gentleness and respect" (1 Peter 3:15).

I pray that this will encourage you to look again at what we were saying in the last section about preparing the ground of our hearts in order to be of maximum blessing to others.

SUMMARY

Learning how to be ready at all times for whatever the Lord would want us to do is foundational training for Christian disciples. None of us is exempt from the responsibility of always being willing to share with others the Gospel of peace.

PRAYER

Help me, Lord, to always be alert, to listen to Your voice and to respond quickly when You show me those things that You want me to do. I do not want to miss out on being a blessing to others. In Jesus' name, Amen.

THE **JOY** OF SERVING GOD

This is a very exciting stage of our journey. We will be focusing our attention on the source of real joy and on discovering that the greatest joy any of us can ever experience is found through knowing God as Father. After we determine that fact, we can then discover that joy is maintained from being in relationship with Him and by serving Him in the center of His will.

It is as we allow God to heal our pasts that we get ourselves more in the place where we can both hear His voice clearly and fulfill the destiny that God prepared for us in advance (see Ephesians 2:10). If we are not in a right relationship with Father God, then we will become wise in our own eyes (see Proverbs 3:7) and do our own things. We can then become the judge of what is right or wrong. If that happens, we will start to reap a harvest of unrighteousness rather than the blessing of God.

An unhealed past—especially one that is unhealed because pride will not allow us to face the fact that some of our limitations have been caused by our own sin choices—can be like a pair of spiritual earplugs. They block out the gentle voice of the shepherd when He is trying to get our attention and lead us into green pastures so that He can restore our souls. I wonder how many unrestored souls there are in the Body of Christ because they simply are not in a place where they can hear His voice and do His will?

The Source of Joy

Jonathan Edwards was at the heart of the Great Awakening. It was one of the most significant moves of the Spirit of God in recorded Christian history.

He understood this principle clearly when he said, "Christ is not only a remedy for your weariness and trouble, but he will give you an abundance of the contrary, joy and delight."* Jonathan Edwards saw Christ as both the source of healing (the remedy for your weariness and trouble) and the fountain of joy.

When Moses struck the rock in the wilderness, the situation was grim and desperate. Without water the children of Israel would die. They put him in a bad situation by complaining and testing both him and God. He knew that it was not right to test the Lord in this way, and he knew that they were ready to stone him. Moses also knew, though, that God would not have brought them out of Egypt just to let them die in the desert. His people were not in the same faith position that he was (see Exodus 17:3–4).

This is always the case when people take their eyes off God and put them on a man. Even a leader as great as Moses will have people who will eventually rebel and turn against them. He alone will never be able to fulfill all of their expectations. It is only when our eyes are fixed firmly on God, who is the source of life, that the depth of healing that He longs to give us can be received. As long as people are looking to men or women to be their source of supply, they will always be disappointed.

Moses cried out to God for help, and God answered his cry. He told Moses what to do, saying:

> "Go out in front of the people. Take with you some of the elders of Israel and take in your hand the staff with which you struck the Nile, and go.

*Jonathan Edwards in Henry Rogers, *The Works of Jonathan Edwards, A.M.: With an Essay on His Genius and Writings*, vol. 2 (London: Paternoster-Row, 1829), 935.

I will stand there before you by the rock at Horeb. Strike the rock, and water will come out of it for the people to drink."

Exodus 17:5–6

The rock that Moses struck has always been understood to be a picture of Christ the Rock, who is the source of healing and life and the remedy for weariness and trouble. He must always be the one we come to. God may use others to be His agents of healing, but it is always God in and through Christ Jesus who is the source of that healing. He alone is our source of joy. He is the only one who can keep the spring waters flowing from the very core of our beings.

This is what Jesus said to the woman at the well:

"Everyone who drinks this water will be thirsty again, but whoever drinks the water I give them will never thirst. Indeed, the water I give them will become in them a spring of water welling up to eternal life."

John 4:13–14

This is your source of joy—a spring that does not run dry, regardless of what the circumstances may be.

Joy and Happiness

The Bible is full of references to both joy and rejoicing. People who are rejoicing are expressing the joy that is flowing within them. Paul urges his readers by saying, "Rejoice in the Lord always. I will say it again: Rejoice!" (Philippians 4:4). Christians have good news in their hearts to rejoice about, and Paul is encouraging them to express that joy and not keep it hidden.

This is what David experienced when the Ark of Covenant was brought back to Jerusalem, and he was "leaping and dancing before the LORD" (2 Samuel 6:16). He could not contain his thankful heart. Not everyone was of the same mind as David. Even his wife Michal despised what was happening.

The Joy of Serving God

The Ark of the Covenant represented the presence of God, and its return to Jerusalem was a wonderful Old Testament picture of the presence of God returning to the hearts of man. The presence of God is the source of joy. Joy is an experience that only Christians can understand. It is radically different from happiness, and it can only be reached in and through the presence of God.

A happy person can also be a joyful person, but happiness can be a very superficial experience. It is related to circumstances and is disconnected from the Christian experience of joy.

On the day I was writing this section, the newspaper had photographs of an elderly couple who had won a great sum of money playing the lottery. Not surprisingly, their faces looked really happy in the pictures.

Winning the lottery, however, will not change anything on the inside. When the emotion of the moment wears away, people will soon discover that their big win has not changed them internally. Sometimes the excess of money disrupts the activities of their lives to the extent that they are less happy than before they won.

Happiness that is related to circumstances may be wonderful for a season, but it does not heal a broken heart. It does not cure depression, and it certainly does not bring the healing that comes about through forgiving others.

Someone with depression might enjoy watching his favorite football team play a fantastic game and have a great victory. When the feelings of elation wear off, though, it is possible that the depression could go even deeper. This is true especially if the person realizes that the experience has not made any difference to his underlying condition.

Some people try to gain temporary happiness through alcohol or drugs. Whatever happy feelings they may have during the highs of their experience, when the effects wear off, nothing will have changed. Sometimes people discover that when they were high on drugs or intoxicated with alcohol that they did things that they now regret. Due to these things, their condition is worse than it was before. It may feel great to be happy, but happiness can be a very temporary and unsatisfactory experience.

The Nature of Joy

Joy, on the other hand, is very different from happiness. It is not dependent on circumstances at all. Yes, a joyful person will be even more joyful and feel happy when good things are happening, but a joyful person can still be joyful when good things are not happening. Joy has its root in the spirit of man, whereas happiness has its root in the soul.

The reason is simple—joy is an outworking of how we are in our inner beings. It is a fruit of being in a right relationship with God. That is why joy is included in the fruit that the Holy Spirit develops in our lives (see Galatians 5:22). This means that people can still know joy in their hearts even when circumstances surrounding them are difficult.

Oswald Chambers was a much-loved commentator on the Word of God. He died tragically in Egypt of a ruptured appendix when he was serving as a chaplain in World War I. One of the most popular devotional books ever published was compiled from his writings and sermons. It was called *My Utmost for His Highest*. When commenting on joy, Oswald Chambers put it this way: "The Bible talks plentifully about joy, but it nowhere speaks about a 'happy' Christian. Happiness depends on what happens; joy does not. Remember, Jesus Christ had joy, and He prays 'that they might have My joy fulfilled in themselves.'"*

The supreme example of joy in the midst of suffering is expressed by the writer of the letter to the Hebrews when he said of Jesus that "for the joy set before him he endured the cross, scorning its shame, and sat down at the right hand of the throne of God" (12:2).

Jesus' joy was definitely not because He was happy about the coming events of Calvary. His joy came from a far deeper spring than His immediate circumstances. What His Father had given Him to do was the only thing that motivated Him. That was the origin of the supreme joy that He knew would be His even as He endured the cross.

Sir Wilfred Grenfell, an amazing missionary doctor who opened up the cold wastes of Labrador to the Gospel at the end of the nineteenth

---

*Oswald Chambers, "Biblical Psychology," *The Complete Works of Oswald Chambers* (Grand Rapids: Discovery House, 2000), 171.

century said, "Real joy comes not from ease or riches or from praise of men, but from doing something worthwhile."†

Grenfell's life was lived in some of the most arduous of conditions. He was tested to the very limits of his endurance. But what he accomplished in life resulted in him experiencing the same sort of joy that motivated Jesus—the fulfillment of what Father God had made him for and given him to do. What joy!

For a moment consider what this young man achieved. He went to Oxford University and then trained as a doctor at London University. While he was there, his life was changed forever through the ministry of the great American evangelist D. L. Moody.

Instead of entering into a normal medical practice, Wilfred Grenfell joined the Royal National Mission to Deep Sea Fishermen and pioneered the development of their first hospital ship. He was following the principle of one step at a time, one day at a time, as he sought to follow Jesus into his ultimate destiny. These were stepping stones along the way.

This work took him to Labrador in 1892, where he was shocked greatly by what he later described as "the poverty and ignorance and semi-starvation among English speaking people of our own race."‡ He decided to devote the rest of his life to improving the lives of the people of Labrador.

In 1893 he established the first hospital at Battle Harbour. It came to be known as the Labrador Medical Mission. As time went on, he not only built other hospitals, but also opened nursing stations, schools, orphanages and social welfare centers.

When he retired over forty years later, he had built an organization that included six hospitals, seven nursing stations, four hospital ships, four boarding schools, fourteen industrial centers, twelve clothing distribution centers, a co-operative lumber mill and a seaman's institute at Saint John's, Newfoundland.

†Wilfred Grenfell, "Wilfred Thomason Grenfell > Quotes," Goodreads, https://www.goodreads.com/author/quotes/14943724.Wilfred_Thomason_Grenfell.

‡Wilfred Grenfell, "Dr. Sir Wilfred Grenfell (1865–1940)," *Grenfell Family History*, http://www.grenfellhistory.co.uk/biographies/wilfred_thomason_grenfell.php.

It would be difficult to exaggerate what his lifework meant to the people of Labrador as an example of practical Christianity. It reached all of the ethnic groups. His joy was certainly full. There is truly no limit to what one life that is totally sold out to Jesus Christ can achieve for the Kingdom of God.

Nehemiah's Joy

Perhaps the most well-known Bible reference to joy comes in the epic saga of how Nehemiah heard the voice of the Lord while still a prisoner of war and a wine waiter to King Artaxerxes. His grief over the broken-down walls and gates of Jerusalem turned into intercession. As a result, he gained permission from the king to return to Jerusalem to rebuild the wall. He accomplished this feat in spite of great opposition in 52 days.

When the wall was finished, Ezra the scribe brought out the Law of the Lord and read it to the people (see Nehemiah 8:1). The Levites were asked to explain its meaning so that the people would understand the Law and know what to do with the information they heard (see Nehemiah 8:8).

As a result of hearing and understanding the Law, the people came under conviction for their sin and began to weep. The next chapter describes more of what was going on as the people confessed both their sins and the wickedness of their fathers, after which they spent a quarter of the day in confession and worship (see Nehemiah 9:2–3).

This was one of those extraordinary moments in the history of a people of God that turned out to be a day (or several days) of tears of repentance intermingled with tears of joy. For where there is true confession, repentance and forgiveness, there will always be deep-seated joy. Both Ezra and Nehemiah caught the mood of God in what they said to the people. Ezra said, "This day is holy to the Lord your God. Do not mourn or weep" (Nehemiah 8:9). Nehemiah said, "Do not grieve, for the joy of the Lord is your strength" (Nehemiah 8:10).

The people understood that days of confession and repentance are ultimately days of joy, celebration and thanksgiving, because the people once again have come close to the heart of God, and He is rejoicing with them. "Then all the people went away to eat and drink, to send portions of food [to those who had nothing prepared] and to celebrate with great joy, because they now understood the words that had been made known to them" (Nehemiah 8:12).

If you could take before and after group photos of the people on one of our Healing Retreats, you would see the scene in Nehemiah unfolding before your eyes. The teaching on these retreats often opens the eyes of the people to things they have never understood before. They are then able to deal with their issues, and the joy of the Lord in their hearts is the result. The looks on their faces tell the whole story.

It is this joy that Nehemiah says is our strength. It is a joy that no one and nothing can ever take away. It is not a joy that is dependent on circumstances. It is a joy that radiates from the heart of God into the heart of man.

When the people of God understand this message, it is totally life transforming. I would go so far as to say that unless they understand this message, they will always fall short of God's best for their lives.

When we apply the Word of God to our lives, we are able to receive God's healing for the damage we have sustained from the things that we have done. We also receive healing for the consequences of wounds we have received as a result of what others have done to us. The effect is nothing short of miraculous.

Twin Joys—Double Strength

There are two joys that God wants us to celebrate. There is the joy that comes from knowing Father God and having His order established in our lives through the application of His truth (the Nehemiah joy), and there is the joy that comes from then getting into the place of serving God as He leads us.

When we know this double joy, we can smile through the circumstances around us and rejoice in the Lord always, as Paul told us to do. The joy of the Lord in the hearts of believers produces disciples who are true overcomers. It produces people who face mountains and do not let them become obstacles, and people who see the opposition but do not flinch as they walk through the crowd into their destinies in God.

I pray that as you gradually absorb the truths of God's Word in your daily walk through the pages of Journey to Freedom, you will not only be able to lift up your eyes and look on the fields that are white for harvest, but you will also be able to press through in God to take your part in God's team of disciples doing the works of the Kingdom.

SUMMARY

If we are in a place of joy, we are also in a place of strength. God wants us to experience the joy of relationship with Him. Through that relationship, He wants us to know the joy of healing in our hearts and of serving Him in the fields of the Kingdom of God. The greatest joy any of us can ever have comes through knowing God as Father and being in the center of His will for our lives.

PRAYER

Thank You, Lord, that You also rejoice when Your children are able to rejoice. Help me to live in such a way that I will not ever move out of that place where I daily experience the strengthening of Your joy in my heart. In Jesus' name, Amen.

NOW READ ON . . .

Congratulations on completing this first and vital step on your personal journey to freedom. I pray that the foundational truths from God's Word that we have shared together in *Building on the Rock* will become anchored in your spirit and will equip you for your journey of life.

In book two, *God, Me and the Enemy*, we will learn much more about the nature and character of God, about ourselves and about how Satan, the enemy of souls, seeks to undermine our faith and lead us away from the truth. Knowing God as He really is and understanding ourselves is vital to our personal journeys of healing and restoration. The apostle Paul reminded us how important it is not to be ignorant of how Satan operates and opposes the life of a believer (see 2 Corinthians 2:11).

May I encourage you now to persevere in your faith with what Paul said: "I press on to take hold of that for which Christ Jesus took hold of me" (Philippians 3:12).

God has given each of us a purpose in life, and as you continue on your journey to freedom with book two, I pray that you will be strengthened to press on toward this goal.

"Let us throw off everything that hinders and the sin that so easily entangles. And let us run with perseverance the race marked out for us, fixing our eyes on Jesus" (Hebrews 12:1–2).

Peter Horrobin is the founder and international director of Ellel Ministries. Ellel Ministries was first established in 1986 as a ministry of healing in northwest England. Many lives were transformed through what God was doing, and the ministry could not be contained in one location. In the early nineties, the work quickly expanded to other parts of the country and into eastern Europe. Today the ministry is established in well over 50 operational centers in over 35 different countries.

Peter was born in 1943 in Bolton, Lancashire, and was brought up in Blackburn, also in Northern England. His parents gave him a firm Christian foundation with a strong evangelical emphasis. His early grounding in the Scriptures would equip him for future ministry.

After graduating from Oxford University with a degree in chemistry, he spent a number of years lecturing in colleges and universities. He transitioned from the academic environment to the world of business, where he founded a series of successful publishing and bookselling companies.

In his twenties, Peter started to restore a vintage sports car (an Alvis Speed 20) but discovered that its chassis was bent. As he looked at the wreck of his broken car, wondering if it could ever be repaired, he sensed God saying, *You can restore this broken car, but I can restore broken lives. Which is more important?* It was obvious that broken lives were more important than broken cars, so the vision for restoring the lives of people was birthed in Peter's heart.

A few years later, he was asked to help a person who had been sexually abused. Through this experience, God further opened up to him the vision of a healing ministry. He prayed daily into this vision until 1986 when God brought it into being. Ellel Grange, a country house just outside the city of Lancaster, provided the first home and the name of

Ellel Ministries. Many Christian leaders affirmed the vision and gave it their support. Since then, a hallmark of Peter's ministry has been his willingness to step out in faith to see God move to fulfil His promises, often in remarkable ways.

Under Peter and his wife's leadership, the worldwide teaching and ministry team has seen God move dramatically in many people's lives to bring salvation, hope, healing and deliverance. Together Peter and Fiona teach and minister on many different aspects of healing and discipleship. Ellel Ministries operates by faith and depends on donations and income from training courses to maintain and expand the work.

Outside of Ellel Ministries, Peter was the originator and one of the compilers of the amazingly successful and popular *Mission Praise*, now in its thirtieth anniversary edition (HarperCollins, 2015). It was originally compiled for Billy Graham's Mission England in 1984.

The story of Peter's life and of how God built and extended the ministry is told in his book *Strands of Destiny* (Sovereign World, 2018). He describes many of the extraordinary and miraculous events through which God has sustained the ministry across the years. JOURNEY TO FREEDOM is a culmination of over thirty years of experience teaching the foundational principles of healing and discipleship and ministering to people all over the world.

For details about the current worldwide activities of Ellel Ministries International, please go to www.ellel.org.

www.ingramcontent.com/pod-product-compliance
Lightning Source LLC
Chambersburg PA
CBHW070838160426
43192CB00012B/2236